Torn

By the same author

Helpless

Trapped

A Small Boy's Cry (e-short)

Two More Sleeps (e-short)

Betrayed

Unexpected (e-short)

ROSIE LEWIS

A terrified girl.

A shocking secret.

A terrible choice.

Certain details in this story, including names, places and dates, have been changed to protect the family's privacy.

HarperElement
An imprint of HarperCollins*Publishers*
1 London Bridge Street
London SE1 9GF

www.harpercollins.co.uk

First published by HarperElement 2016

1 3 5 7 9 10 8 6 4 2

A catalogue record of this book is
available from the British Library

PB ISBN 978-0-00-811297-4
EB ISBN 978-0-00-811298-1

362.733092

Printed and bound in Great Britain by
Clays Ltd, St Ives plc

MIX
Paper from
responsible sources
FSC www.fsc.org **FSC° C007454**

Prologue

Taylor hates weekends.

All she keeps whispering, over and over as she tiptoes around the house, is, 'Come on, Monday, please come on.' She doesn't think anyone in the whole world wants Saturday to be over as much as she does. Dad's eyes are on fire, like they're about to explode. Mum's lips have been white all day, pinched together like when there's a sad bit on the news. She keeps picking things up, looking confused and then putting them down again.

Taylor knows something bad is going to happen; she can always tell. She glances from Dad to Mum, trying not to catch a glimpse of the spots of red on the carpet – her tummy goes funny when she remembers how they got there. Her little brother, Reece, huddles next to her on the sofa, his knees scrunched right up to his chin. He's been crazy all day, grovelling around everyone and trying to please them. It makes Taylor sick.

She can't wait to go to bed but it's not even six o'clock. Jimmy, their Labrador, pads over and rests his chin on her lap. Every time one of them moves the puppy makes a noise, a sort of cross between a growl and a whimper. Taylor buries her face into his soft fur and cups her hand over his muzzle. 'Shush, there's a good boy, shush.' When she looks up she sees that Mum has stopped tidying. She's standing in front of them, a strange look on her face.

Taylor's heart beats faster.

Dad hovers and, moving in slow motion, Mum starts tidying again, even though there's nothing left to put away. Reece rubs his nose and sniffs. Taylor can feel his leg trembling.

Her eyes skirt slowly around the room. Things are definitely about to blow, she can feel it. Pretending to be calm, she tries to plan an escape route in her head like that girl in the *Hideout* cartoon, but it's much harder than the website makes out. The front door is locked and she doesn't know where the keys are. It occurs to her that one of the windows upstairs might be open, but then she remembers that Bailey is still in his cot and there's no way she's going to make a run for it without her baby brother. Oh, why can't she think of something?

The wind blows outside the window and Taylor hears a clomping sound: footsteps on the pavement. Someone is walking past their house like none of this is going on. How can things carry on as normal, Taylor wonders, when everything is *so* wrong? Jimmy hears it too. His ears prick up and he jumps to his feet, barking. Mum's head shoots round. Reece's knees knock together.

For one hopeful second Taylor considers calling out for help but Jimmy starts howling and she freezes. His tail is buried so far between his legs that she can hardly see it. Keeping Mum in sight, Taylor edges closer to Jimmy and wraps her arms around his neck. 'Please, Jimmy,' she whispers, 'it's all right. Please don't.'

Jimmy pulls away. He leaps around in circles, snapping at the air. Mum sways on her feet, her eyes flitting over the three of them. Taylor knows one of them is about to pay but she isn't about to stand by and let her family get hurt, not again. She's ten years old now and she's been learning how to fight.

Ignoring the sick feeling in her tummy, she takes a deep breath and forces herself to her feet.

Chapter One

Maisie Stone eased the end of a biro between the wiry roots of her thick auburn dreadlocks, half-closing one eye as she twirled it around. Turning the radio on to mask our conversation, I reflected that the social worker wasn't exactly what I'd envisaged when we'd spoken earlier that day, but then neither were the siblings waiting miserably upstairs in the spare room.

'So, Rosie, this is kind of awkward,' Maisie lisped, the words rolling over her silver-studded tongue so slowly that it was as if she needed winding up. Over the telephone she had spoken with such slow deliberateness that in my head she was nearing retirement. The woman sitting in front of me, with a thin leather bandana tied around her hair and taffeta skirt skimming her sandalled feet, had taken me completely by surprise. With her full lips and wide green eyes, there was an earthy appeal about Maisie, but the skin beneath her eyes was swollen and dotted with blemishes.

By the way she was dressed I guessed she was in her early thirties at most, but somehow she seemed much older. Either that or she hadn't slept in days. 'When I picked them up I couldn't believe there was one of each.'

'You'd never met them before?'

Maisie's beaded dreadlocks jingled as she shook her head. 'No, their file landed on my desk at half past ten this morning. I only had time for, like, a quick flick through and when I saw Taylor described as a massive Chelsea fan I just assumed, what with her name and everything –' her words trailed away and then she groaned, pulling her hands down her face. 'Is there any way you could, like, jiggle things around to make it work?'

It was the look of open appeal on her face that really got my sympathy going. 'Well, maybe there is a way,' I said, my mind still clawing through possible solutions as I spoke. According to my fostering agency's rules, only the under-fives or same-sex siblings were allowed to share a room. Since Taylor and Reece fitted neither category, they needed a foster carer with two spare bedrooms.

'And you're sure you don't mind?' Maisie asked a few minutes later, her eyes, if not bright with relief, then at least a little less puffy than they had been.

'Oh, it's not really a problem,' I answered, in a not quite convincing tone. I wanted to help and so had offered to convert our dining room into a temporary bedroom for myself. On a practical level it made sense – Taylor and Reece were already here and it was a bit late in the day to start hunting for a new placement for them – but the thought of dismantling the dining table and then dragging my own double bed downstairs wasn't very appealing.

'Cool,' the social worker said, the thick wooden bangles on her wrists knocking together as she scratched the other side of her scalp. 'We prefer children to stay at their own school if at all possible, and the only other carer matching their profile lives, like, forty miles away.'

'Ah, I see,' I said, my eyes narrowing. When social workers were desperate to place children, all sorts of cunning ruses came into play. I was beginning to wonder whether there really had been a mix-up over Taylor's sex when the rise and fall of frenzied conversation drifted down the stairs. The noise brought my thoughts firmly back to the children and I decided to focus on the positives. With a nationwide shortage of foster carers, siblings were still sometimes separated. At least, in this instance, they could stay together. The base of my bed came in two halves so hopefully it wouldn't be too heavy to lift and, compared with the upheaval Taylor and Reece were going through, moving a bit of furniture wasn't too much of a hardship. 'What's their history?' I asked, setting my suspicions aside. I knew that five-year-old Reece had made a disclosure to his teacher earlier that day, but that was about all.

Maisie blinked several times. She seemed to be struggling to summon the energy to speak. 'So, as I said, I haven't had a chance to go through their entire file yet but it seems that the children have been registered as "in need" for years. Their regular social worker is on long-term sick and I've only just inherited the case, but from what I can make out, a few incidents of domestic violence have been flagged up to us by police. Nothing too serious, but Dad is long-term unemployed and when you add Mum's depression into the mix –'

Maisie's sentence trailed off and I nodded, unsurprised. It was the spring of 2005 and although I had only been fostering for a couple of years, I had already noticed a common theme of domestic violence among the families of looked-after children. The violence was often accompanied by parental depression and substance abuse, a set of issues labelled by social workers as 'the toxic trio'. When all three 'markers' were present, children were feared to be most at risk of severe harm.

'Unfortunately, Taylor, the eldest, has been replicating the violence at school,' Maisie said, snail-like. 'I'm told that most of her classmates want nothing to do with her.'

'Oh dear,' I said, pressing my lips together. It was natural for Taylor to use her personal experiences as a template for relating to others. The poor girl was probably suffering as much as the children she was bullying, although I knew that was a view that could be unpopular, particularly with parents of the victim.

Maisie leaned back into the sofa and sipped from a can of Red Bull. It was her second since she'd arrived and I couldn't help but wonder what she would be like without all that caffeine, if this was Maisie on fire. 'As you probably know, Rosie, we have a duty of care to keep children within their own family if at all possible. It looks like all sorts of intervention therapies have been offered but the Fieldings have refused to engage with any of them.'

Longing to get upstairs and help the children to settle in, I reached for the nearest cushion, planted it on my lap and fiddled with the tassels. Being plucked from one life and planted in another one was a shock for anyone and the siblings were probably still reeling. Of course, there were some things that Maisie needed to tell me in private, but her drawl was agonisingly slow. 'What did Reece disclose?'

'So, Reece's teacher noticed a red mark on his thigh as the class were changing for PE this morning. At first he made out that he'd been stung –'

I grimaced, amazed at the lengths children went to in defending parents who offered little protection in return.

'I know, sweet, yeah? But when pressed, he admitted that his mother had slapped him. Mum's insisting that it was just a little tap but there's a mark, like,' Maisie cupped her hands together in the shape of a rugby ball, 'this big on his thigh.'

I sighed, my heart going out to him. It was March and the Easter holidays were only a few days away. There was often an influx of children coming into care when school holidays loomed – children seemed more able to cope with problems at home with the daily security of school to escape to but the prospect of losing that safety net some-times drove them to reach out to their teachers for help. As a consequence, more disclosures were made in July and December than at any other time of the year.

'School says that Mum's really dedicated to the children so we're leaving Bailey with her for the moment. There have been concerns about him since birth, mainly due to Mum's mental health issues, but she's on medication for her depression and things have been stable for a while, until this happened of course. We're going to need to keep a close eye on things.'

'Bailey?'

'Oh, yeah, course, you don't know that yet. He's the youngest, fifteen months or so.' Maisie took another sip of the energy drink. 'We're holding an emergency strategy meeting tomorrow to discuss what to do about him. For now, the parents have agreed to a Section 20 for Taylor and Reece.'

If children were removed from their parents under a Section 20, Voluntary Care Order, their parents retained full rights, at liberty to withdraw consent to foster care at any time. Reluctant families sometimes went along with a voluntary plan because they felt that they had more control over what happened to their children.

As Maisie finished her drink, I found myself wishing I had more space at home so that little Bailey could join us, should he need to come into care. Having recently attended a child protection course, I knew that on average over the past two years in the UK, more than one child a week lost their life at the hands of a violent parent. It seemed to me that social workers had a delicate balancing act on their hands in trying to ensure that the welfare of the child was paramount.

Torn

One of Douglas Adams's dictums suddenly came to me. He said, 'The fact that we live at the bottom of a deep gravity well, on the surface of a gas-covered planet going around a nuclear fireball 90 million miles away and think this to be normal is obviously some indication of how skewed our perspective tends to be.' When a child is taken into care, the course of their life is sometimes changed for ever and I've often wondered how social workers set the bar of negligence objectively, in the absence of a definitive answer. I was just glad that the task of making such far-reaching decisions was outside of the remit of a foster carer's role.

A loud scream from upstairs interrupted my thoughts. Maisie blinked and looked at me. I jumped to my feet and ran into the hall. 'Are you all right up there?' I called, taking the stairs two at a time.

Chapter Two

'It weren't me,' Taylor said, touching her hand to her chest.
Straight away my eyes were drawn to her fingernails,
painted a dazzling strawberry red. Sitting on the single bed
nearest the door, she flicked her waist-length, burnished
blonde hair over one shoulder and blinked belligerently.
Five-year-old Reece, whey-faced and hesitant, hovered in
the middle of the room chewing his bottom lip. 'W-w-what's
going on? Where we sleeping?' he asked, his face a picture
of uncertainty. He dragged a knuckle across one eye,
dislodging the black-rimmed spectacles he wore so that
they fell across his cheek. 'W-w-where's Mummy?'

'Well, that's what Maisie and I have been discussing,' I
said, the disembodied screams already drifting to the back
of my mind. The social worker entered the room at that
moment, stopping just inside the door. She rested her back
against the wall with a sigh, as if the task of climbing the
stairs had drained the last dregs of her energy. 'We've

decided that, Reece, you can have this room and, Taylor,' I turned to the ten-year-old, 'you'll be in a room just down the hall. I expect Maisie will fill you in on when you can see your mum. Isn't that right, Maisie?'

She nodded. 'Yeah, sure. That's something I need to discuss with Mummy first though.'

'But there are t-t-two beds in here,' Reece said, screwing his eyes up and then blinking rapidly in what appeared to be a nervous twitch. 'What one's mine?'

'Either one,' I told him, smiling reassuringly. 'We'll decide later shall we?'

He looked horrified at that, his mouth falling open in shock. Despite possessing the appearance of a miniature bouncer, with his closely cropped mouse-brown hair, broad forehead and stocky chest, I got the sense that Reece would need lots of reassurance to cope with being thrust into such an unfamiliar situation. 'Tell you what,' I said gently, walking over to the bed beneath the window and perching on the edge. 'This bed is comfy. Would you like to sleep here?'

For a split-second his features relaxed but then his thick eyebrows contracted, his amber-brown eyes pooling with tears. The fine lower lashes glistened, darkening his eye sockets so heavily that they appeared bruised. 'I want Mummy,' he cried, toddler-like. He clutched his midriff. 'Ow, I got a tummy ache now.'

'Aw, I know, honey. It's all a bit overwhelming isn't it?' I held out my hand and he shuffled a few tentative steps towards me, lower lip trembling.

'Oh, for God's sake,' Taylor mumbled, running her fingers through her hair and clamping it in a fist at the top of her head. The V of a sharply defined widow's peak stood on show momentarily, until her hand dropped to her lap, her cheeks ballooning with a loud, huffing breath. Humiliated, Reece froze, mid-step. After a swift glance at his sister, he bent one knee and stretched his arms up over his head, as if he'd been planning to warm up his muscles. Taylor rolled her eyes and lifted her trainer-clad feet onto the bed. I felt a tightening in my stomach – a longing to slip an arm around Reece's shoulder and reassure him that he was safe.

I smiled at him instead and then turned to his sister. 'Not on the sheets please, Taylor.' Still in the infancy of my fostering career, I felt awkward imposing discipline on a child I had only just met, but caring for Alfie, a little boy with a penchant for biting, had honed my conviction that early firmness paid off. When the three-year-old had first arrived at our house, skinny and bruised, I felt such sympathy for him that I had allowed him to rampage through the house unbridled. It took five weeks to regain control, during which time we were all thoroughly miserable. I wasn't about to make the same mistake again.

Taylor tutted and heaved a heavy sigh but, I was relieved to see, kicked her trainers off using the edge of each foot. Sockless, her toenails were painted a deep maroon, the colour complementing her painted fingernails. I lifted my hands up and clapped them softly together. 'Great, thank you. We'll move the bed you're sitting on after we've had dinner and then you can see your room. Is that OK?'

Torn

She lifted one shoulder in a half-hearted shrug and I took a long assessing look at her, trying to work out whether I was sensing an attitude or poorly disguised shyness. Something in her stance emitted an air of reckless disregard and my thoughts were suddenly touched by Riley, a fourteen-year-old lad who came to us as an emergency placement the previous year. Tossed aside by his alcoholic mother and excluded from school, his life before coming into care was disorganised and traumatic, stripped of all that was gentle. New to fostering at the time, it took me a few days to realise that living dangerously close to the edge was Riley's own dysfunctional way of coping with the implacable truth that no one cared. Heartbreak, I came to realise, was most often the cause of bad behaviour.

Riley was only with us for three weeks and moved on to a married couple in their early sixties. I was recently startled to hear them proudly announcing that Riley was studying hard for his GCSEs with the ambition of becoming a police officer as soon as he was old enough. Bearing in mind that Riley used to remove the shells from snails and then set light to them, the transformation was remarkable.

Of slighter build than her brother, Taylor put me in mind of a young Hayley Mills. There was definitely more than a passing resemblance there, in her rosy pout, fair skin sprinkled with freckles and deep-blue eyes. Her clothes were anything but 1950s though – she was wearing a navy velour tracksuit top and tight cropped jeans. Even from across the room I could see that they were expensive.

Physically speaking, it was easy to see that the siblings were related, but the similarities seemed to end there. Where Reece seemed highly strung and agitated, Taylor came across as confident, cocky even. But it was early days and children rarely presented their true selves when surrounded by unfamiliar people. According to Maisie, the siblings had been expecting a late-afternoon shopping trip with their mum. It must have been an unpleasant shock to find an unfamiliar social worker waiting for them in the headmistress's office at the end of the school day. To make matters worse, I had been so surprised to find a boy and girl on my doorstep that my intended warm welcome evaporated as soon as I laid eyes on them. Quickly recovering, I had hoisted a smile back on my face, but, as I was to appreciate in the coming weeks, first impressions stick.

'OK, good.' I turned to Maisie and raised my eyebrows, waiting for some input. Eyes watering, she blinked several times, then looked at me expectantly. I got to my feet. Clearly I was going to have to take the lead. 'Right, shall we go downstairs, then?'

The doorbell rang before I'd reached the bottom stair. Taylor, who had been whispering insistently in her brother's ear since leaving the bedroom, suddenly clamped a protective hand on his shoulder, holding him back. 'Who's that?' she demanded, sounding thoroughly displeased with the unexpected development.

'Emily and Jamie I expect,' I said, glancing back at Taylor. The ghost of a fearful expression lingered on her face. Swiftly, she replaced it with one of disgruntlement but not before I'd noticed. I paused on the stair for a split-second, registering a swell of compassion for her. Beneath her surly exterior was deep unhappiness – I could sense it – no matter how much hubris she managed to project. Reaching it wasn't going to be easy, I was almost certain of that and as I opened the door another thought fleetingly occurred to me – just what had she been drilling her brother about in such an urgent tone? 'Ah, yes, here they are!'

My ex-husband, Gary, stood behind Emily, our daughter, who was ten at the time and our seven-year-old son, Jamie. The air around them was damp with misty rain, the sky a stormy grey.

'Hi,' Gary said, surprising me with his distant tone. After separating three years earlier, when I was thirty-one, our first year apart had been turbulent. Each of us unsure how to behave, we had passed the children awkwardly between us, something we never dreamed would happen when we first held them in our arms. The trouble was, there seemed to be no raft for fledgling divorcees to grasp on to, no chart to navigate our way out of enemy territory. It took a while to find but eventually, with joint relief, we anchored ourselves in a place of calm, even salvaging a friendship of sorts.

Now though, Gary, five years older than me and craggier, in a handsome way, with each passing year, was bobbing from foot to foot as if cold. Craning his neck, he looked beyond me, into the hall. When my gaze drifted over the top of his head, the uncharacteristic formality made sense – his new partner, Debbie, was waiting in the passenger seat of his car, staring towards the house. Debbie was uninvolved in the ending of our marriage but, somehow, in my not quite healed mind, she was guilty by association. Dark haired and attractive, Debbie smiled when our eyes met. I lifted my hand in a wave, about as much interaction as any of us could take, I think, and it was a relief when the light rain escalated into a deluge. Gary, I noticed with stifled amusement, appeared equally thankful. After ruffling Jamie's hair and touching a thumb to Emily's cheek, he dashed off to the car.

Characteristically bypassing introductions, Jamie bundled into the house first, pulling up short at the bottom of the stairs. I had called Gary earlier and asked him to update Emily and Jamie on the placement before they arrived home. They loved being part of a fostering family but I wasn't sure how they'd feel if they found two similarly aged children making themselves comfortable without prior warning. 'You're five,' Jamie told the bewildered boy who had taken my place on the first stair.

Reece screwed his eyes up again and then glanced at his sister, as if checking it was safe to confirm such personal information. Taylor raised her eyebrows a fraction and gave a little shrug, body language Reece seemed to interpret as a green light. He turned back to Jamie and nodded.

'And this is Taylor,' I said, gesturing towards the stairs with a nod. 'She's ten.'

Jamie, wiping drops of rain from his forehead with the back of his hand, was about to respond when Taylor took the lead: 'I can't stand boys,' she said, her lip curled upwards in a nasty sneer. 'I literally hate 'em.'

My son stared at her for a moment then glanced at me with a puzzled expression. 'Um, your greeting could do with a little tweaking, Taylor,' I said, trying to make light of it. 'That's something we're going to have to work on, I think.'

'Wha-t?' Taylor asked. From her tone it was as if I'd suggested that she sprinkle the hallway with rose petals and throw herself at my son's feet in welcome. Still perched on the second stair, she was looking down on me with disdain.

'We'll discuss it later,' I told her. Jamie, seemingly unaffected by Taylor's emphatic declaration, plonked his school bag at my feet and scooted off to the living room. Clearly expecting his new, less frosty housemate to follow, he called out, 'What year are you in?' Reece, who seemed to have forgotten all about his tummy ache, trotted after Jamie.

'One,' he shouted behind us, repeating it several times until Jamie made a noise of acknowledgement.

In the living room, Jamie had already separated some Lego into two piles and was directing Reece to start work on the base of a helicopter. Maisie took a seat behind them on the sofa, her gladiator sandals almost touching one of the empty cans of Red Bull lying on the carpet. Emily, her blonde hair glistening with rain, hovered uncertainly at the door. Her eyes followed Taylor with interest as the ten-year-old strode from room to room. My chest tightened as Taylor sat herself down in front of the computer and switched it on without even asking. It was natural for her to want to explore her new surroundings but there was something proprietary in her manner that irked me. It was difficult to imagine Taylor and Emily hitting it off as Jamie and Reece already seemed to have done – Emily was quite a gentle soul and I got the sense that Taylor was a girl who liked to rule the roost.

I was about to tell Taylor that she needed to check with me before using the computer when Maisie held out some papers on a clipboard. When children come into care, their foster carer is expected to sign a placement agreement; a form setting out what is required of them as well as essential information about the children, medical consents and contact arrangements. Since the placement had been arranged in a hurry, much of the form was still blank. After scribbling my signature at the bottom of the last page, a noise from the kitchen drew my attention. Taylor had sauntered past us and opened the fridge. She was standing in front of it, perusing the contents. 'Oh, Taylor, what are you looking for?'

'Food,' she said with a sniff. 'God, isn't that obvious?' she added, her head so far into the fridge that her voice was muffled.

'OK, but tell you what – you let me know what you'd like and I'll get it for you.' I balanced the clipboard on top of a bookshelf and walked through to the kitchen. 'Excuse me please, love,' I said mildly, ignoring her icy stare. 'Would anyone else like a biscuit or something? Maisie? Tea, coffee?'

For the first time since her arrival, Maisie seemed alert. 'Nothing for me thanks,' she said slowly, sitting forwards on the sofa. She was watching us avidly and half an hour later, as the social worker roused herself to leave, I discovered why. 'OK, so, can I just ask you something, Rosie?' she said as she stood in the hall, lifting a large, embroidered handbag and resting the strap on her shoulder.

'Yes, of course.'

'Cool,' she licked her lips, 'so, it's about what happened just now …'

I tilted my chin, trying to work out what she was referring to. I shook my head. 'Sorry, I don't follow.'

'Well, you seemed re-luc-tant for Taylor to have a snack.' She strung each syllable out with agonising slowness. 'Was there – a prob-lem?'

'Oh – of course not, I – no, not at all,' I rushed to explain. Embarrassed, I ran my hand through my long fringe, pulling it back. 'It's just that I'd prefer the children to ask me first if they want something from the fridge.'

Consternation clouded her face, her lips falling open to reveal her tongue stud. It glinted silver against her teeth. 'But you can't limit a child's food intake, Ro-sie.'

Mortified, I hesitated for a moment before answering. 'No, and I never would, not unless there was a problem like obesity or something. But I don't feel they should help themselves to food willy-nilly. My own children have always checked with me first, in case dinner's almost ready or something. It's just the way we do things.'

Maisie's brow furrowed with concern. 'D'you know what, Rosie? I'm an advocate of child-led caring. Children should be able to be free to express themselves and show us what they want,' she said. 'Do you see where I'm coming from?'

'Erm,' I said, suddenly convinced that Maisie was a social worker I would need to tread carefully around. 'Y-es, I believe in doing my best for children as well, absolutely, of course I do. But,' I paused again, searching for a polite but firm response, 'I don't think that necessarily means *always* giving them what they want.'

Maisie wrinkled her nose in a look of distaste, as if I'd waved a soiled nappy in front of her. I worried then about just how far Maisie's commitment to 'child-led caring' might go.

Chapter Three

Back in the living room, Jamie and Reece were clutching their tummies, each convulsed in a fit of giggles.

'What's so funny?' I asked, pleased to see that Reece was looking more relaxed.

Jamie, still snorting, opened his mouth to speak but Taylor, who was seated back at the computer, beat him to it. 'He,' she waved a thumb in my son's direction, 'reckons that that woman stinks. Reece seems to think he's hilarious. It's literally pathetic.'

I glanced between the three of them, wondering where to start. Jamie held his breath, eyeing me sheepishly. 'I – I didn't say she stinks, Mummy,' he said, throwing Taylor a resentful look. She jutted her chin in sneering satisfaction. 'I said she's a bit smelly.'

Reece cupped a giggle in his hand.

'Jamie, how many times have I asked you not to make personal comments unless you have something nice to say?'

I said chidingly. I had noticed that Maisie smelt mildly of cigarettes, and Jamie, being asthmatic, was probably more sensitive to it than the rest of us. He did have a tendency to blurt out whatever thoughts were running through his mind but what he said usually had some basis to it: there was certainly no malice in him. I was just glad he had waited until after she left to mention it.

He bobbed his head then looked up at me earnestly. 'About seventeen?'

I sighed. Taylor, who was lifting the mouse and banging it down on the desk instead of clicking it, snorted. The site she had visited was unrecognisable to me but a stream of conversation was juddering up the screen. 'I'd be grateful if you wouldn't tell tales, Taylor. And is that a chatroom you're in?'

She tossed her head to the side so that her long, poker-straight fringe flew out in an arc and over one shoulder. Her hands then flattened it against her ears, something I had noticed her doing several times since her arrival. 'Fuck off. I wasn't telling tales, he really said it. And it's not no chatroom, der brain, it's Myspace.'

Emily, who had been watching us silently from the corner of the room, gasped at Taylor's attitude. Jamie goggled, staring at me to gauge my reaction. I restrained myself, forcing a mild response. It wasn't unusual for children with no experience of a loving home and its usual boundaries to swear and, though often it was an unconscious habit, sometimes they did it for shock value. 'Um, I think now may be the perfect time to run through some of our house rules,' I said calmly as I crossed the room to open a side cabinet drawer.

Whenever a new child came to stay with us, one of my priorities was to make them feel safe and at ease. Being presented with a set of house rules wasn't the warmest way to welcome someone into our home and so usually I introduced them gradually, reserving the first day for showing them where everything was and finding out what foods they liked. In Taylor's case, I got the feeling it was a case of the sooner the better; she needed to know what was expected of her.

Every household has its own set of basic rules and some children, if they've been moved around in the care system, genuinely find it difficult to keep track of what they can and can't do. It was a simple list –

No hitting

No swearing

No shouting

No going into other people's bedrooms

Everyone makes their own bed each morning

– and one intended to let everyone know where they stood; that was the theory at least.

'Well, I ain't making my own bed for a start,' Taylor mumbled after disdainfully chucking her copy on the floor.

'I want all of us to feel safe in this house,' I said after a moment, ignoring Taylor's heckling and directing my words at everyone. 'And to feel safe we must follow the rules. That means everyone, including me. Do you all understand?'

Emily, Jamie and Reece nodded in unison. Taylor swung her foot and wittered on under her breath.

'Taylor? You OK with that?'

'Meh,' she said, shrugging. 'What y'gonna do?'

I stared at her, my hackles rising. It was nearing 6 o'clock and the prospect of moving several heavy pieces of furniture around was pressing on my thoughts. With a lethal combination of tiredness and hunger beginning to set in as well, I thought it would be wisest to ignore her.

Dinner was thrown together in a hurry – pasta with cheese sauce and garlic bread – one of the few meals that had featured on both Taylor and Reece's lists of favourite foods. Emily and Jamie, who had already eaten with their dad, sat with us at the table while we ate, sipping at mugs of warm milk. It was nice that they wanted to be part of things and I was pleased to see that Taylor and Reece were tucking into their food. Some children lose their appetite after the trauma of separation from their parents but the siblings were scoffing their dinner hungrily, licking stray flakes of parsley from their fingers after each bite of garlic bread. 'Can I have some more, Rosie?' Reece asked thickly, before he'd swallowed his last mouthful. Almost upsetting his beaker of water as he cluttered his knife and fork to the table, he still seemed ill at ease, but it was reassuring to know that at least he had some warm food inside him.

'Yes, of course you can.' A bowl of leftovers sat on a hessian mat in the middle of the table, a long silver serving spoon resting on the rim. 'Help yourself, love,' I said, lowering my own fork and edging the bowl towards him with my fingertips. He raised his eyebrows, surprised it seemed, to be given such a responsibility. I started eating again, nodding encouragingly as he loaded the spoon with pasta and plopped a large dollop onto his plate. He looked up at me and beamed.

'Taylor, would you like some more?' I asked, breaking off a piece of garlic bread for myself. She had taken umbrage at not being allowed a fizzy drink with her meal, something her mum *always* gave her. The resultant scowl was still in place.

Rolling her lips in on themselves, as if she'd just applied a layer of lipstick, she hitched one shoulder up to her ear. 'Meh, tastes like crap if I'm honest.'

Emily's mug froze an inch from her mouth, her eyes darting to meet mine.

'I'd rather you just said you didn't like it, Taylor,' I told her, my voice off-key. Sudden tiredness had drained my desire to remind her of the house rules or embark on a lecture.

She looked at me and shrugged. 'Actually, Reece, stick some more on there then,' she said to her brother, holding her knife and fork to one side to accommodate. 'May as well 'ave some while you're at it.'

Hastily swallowing my mouthful, I said, 'No, Taylor, no more, not if you don't like it. If you're still hungry after you've finished what's on your plate you can have a piece of fruit instead.'

Livid, she coloured at once, her cheeks flame red. Her eyes flitted around the room as if trying to conjure a retort but it seemed she couldn't think of one. She stabbed a piece of pasta with her fork instead, snapping at it with fury as she thrust it into her mouth. For the next few minutes I listened in silence as Emily and Jamie told me about their day, aware that Reece hadn't taken his eyes off me since I'd spoken to his sister. With his head angled slightly to the side, it was as if he was analysing me, trying to gauge my mood. I wasn't sure why – my tone with Taylor had been firm but not fierce. Every so often I threw a smile his way, trying to reassure him that all was well. He reciprocated with an instinctive smile but each time my gaze wandered he grew serious again, the inspection continuing.

When Emily and Jamie mentioned their meal I was tempted to ask them what they thought of Debbie – it was the first time they'd been introduced to her – but I quickly decided it wasn't fair to quiz them, and certainly not in front of Taylor and Reece. I gave myself an imaginary pat on the back for my maturity and my earlier composure. Sometimes I didn't feel all that mature; actually, there were still times when I marvelled that they let me foster at all.

'Who was that man what brought you home?' Reece asked Jamie, his mouth full of garlic bread.

'My dad,' Jamie told him. 'He took us out for pizza.'

'Where'd he go then? Has he gone back to work?'

Jamie's gaze dropped to his lap and my stomach lurched. Of the pair of them, Jamie seemed to be the one who missed his father the most. A few weeks earlier, after visiting a friend who lived with his parents in a beautiful house by the river, Jamie had arrived home full of excitement.

'Mum!' he'd said in urgent, excited tones. 'I've got a great idea. If you and Dad make up, we can all live together in a house like Max.' The expression of hope shining bright in his eyes almost broke my heart.

After an uncomfortable pause I said: 'Emily and Jamie's dad lives in a flat not far from here. You'll meet him soon I expect.'

'Why don't he live here then?' Taylor demanded in an interrogative tone, fixing Emily and Jamie with a stony glare.

I paused, mid-chew. Emily and Jamie, frozen, looked at me in mute appeal. 'I'd rather not discuss it with you, Taylor,' I said, lowering my cutlery to the table and wiping my hands on a piece of kitchen towel. It was a struggle to maintain the mild air that I had instinctively adopted since her arrival.

Silence hung in the air like thick fog, the children glancing uneasily between each other. Taylor, her flush deepening, turned her eyes on me and tilted her head. 'Is it because you're a shit cook?' she asked, delivering the question with a few innocent blinks.

The rain was still hammering down late into the evening, when all the furniture had been moved and everyone was settled in bed. After locking up I padded through to the dining room, where my mattress sagged against the wall looking every bit as weary as I felt. The base of my bed lay in two halves against the fireplace, duvet and pillows in a heap on the table in the middle of the room.

With a hyperactive edge that gave me the jitters, Reece had shadowed me while I lifted and carried, moving obstacles out of my way whenever I drew near. He had tried his best to help, bless him, and though I found his over-eagerness to please a little disconcerting, there was something sweetly old-fashioned about him that I couldn't help but find endearing. But it was as he was getting ready for bed that my heart really went out to him. Bobbing around on his heels, his eyes screwed up into small balls, he had seemed so nervous that my own stomach churned in sympathy. At first I thought his anguish must be homesickness, but then after several circuits of his room he blurted out: 'Have you got any nappies, Rosie? I might wet the bed.' His relief was palpable when I took him to the airing cupboard and showed him my stock of nappies in various sizes. 'Phew, I was that worried, Rosie, I thought I was going to have a heart attack,' he had said, hand clamped to his chest. With his bygone clichés and earnest expressions, it was almost as if he'd strolled out from the pages of a children's storybook.

Taylor's persona, on the other hand, was less Pollyanna, more Stephen King's Carrie. She was only a child but there was something about her that made me feel uneasy. I wasn't sure it was all down to her brittle manner either. Sinking down on one of the hard-backed dining chairs with a sigh, I watched as heavy droplets of rain swam down the misty glass, reflecting gloomily on the way I had handled Taylor's earlier comment. Caught off-guard by the spitefulness of her question and, though it pains me to admit it, irrationally hurt, I had lost my patience and dragged her plate away, telling her to leave the table immediately.

When I attended the initial foster-carer training course three years earlier, not a single social worker had mentioned that foster carers need to develop a really thick skin. Caught between abusive parents, stressed-out children and occasionally insensitive social workers, the role was not ideal for shrinking violets or anyone with even the mildest inferiority complex. I had a feeling that living with Taylor would challenge my own tendency to avoid confrontation; it was going to be a case of sink or swim.

I sighed, disappointed in myself because deep down I knew that part of the problem was my own lack of experience. My reaction had nothing to do with Taylor's comment about my cooking; I wasn't *that* precious. But what had really got my goat, if I'm honest, apart from being irritated by Taylor's assumption that my private life was up for discussion, was that she seemed to have effortlessly located my Achilles heel. Sometimes worried about the effect our divorce might have on Emily and Jamie, I *was* still sensitive about it. The trouble was that by reacting badly I had given Taylor carte blanche to wind me up, whenever she felt she needed to let off steam.

Sullen, provocative and cunningly astute, the ten-year-old certainly seemed nothing like her brother. And yet as I had shown her into her new bedroom and said goodnight, I sensed hesitancy there – a brief moment of candour in her body language that showed me she was close to reaching out, if not for comfort then at least reassurance. Of course, as soon as I took a step towards her she shrank away, as I'd suspected she would.

With a soft groan I forced myself to my feet, telling myself that things would quickly improve. Taylor was probably overwrought with all the emotion of the day and it was inevitable that I, as the nearest adult, would bear the brunt of it. Somehow though, I couldn't quite convince myself that everything would work out fine.

There was often a mixture of emotions at the beginning of a new placement; anxiety of course and trepidation, usually overridden by plenty of excitement. But as I heaved the dining table onto its side and began unscrewing the legs, I was tingling with the feeling, a presentiment almost, that things were going to get a whole lot worse.

What I didn't realise, at the time, was that by accepting the placement I was putting my own family directly in harm's way.

Chapter Four

'Taylor,' I called up the stairs, making an effort to sound as pacific as possible. It was already 8.15 a.m. and with two school runs awaiting execution, I was eager to herd everyone out of the house. Chilled about most things but irrationally petrified of being late, Jamie stood with his hand on the catch of the front door, ready to sprint for the car as soon as Taylor decided to grace us with an appearance. 'We really need to go now, Taylor, or you'll all be late.'

Jamie, bobbing around on the balls of his feet, gave a little squeak of terror.

'Why you indicating?' Taylor demanded from the back of the car, twenty minutes later. 'Our school's straight on.'

'Yes I know, but Devonshire Primary is around here,' I said, throwing her a quick glance over my shoulder as I took a left at the traffic lights.

'Na, you can drop *us* off first,' she said, flicking her right hand at the wrist to gesture a U-turn.

'We discussed this earlier, do you remember?' I asked calmly. While Taylor had been straightening her hair (a task that had taken almost an hour to complete) I told her that we pass Emily and Jamie's school on the way to hers. 'I said that Emily and Jamie will be going in first but in the afternoon we'll do it the other way around, so you'll get first choice of where to sit later on.'

Taylor growled, gesticulating so furiously that Emily, who was sitting next to her, had to shrink away to avoid being slapped. 'Oh-wah! But I need to hand my project in before the bell-errr.' I had noticed that whenever she was annoyed, she prolonged certain words so they ended with an 'er' sound.

'Let's get a wriggle on then,' I said, brightly, checking my teeth in the rear-view mirror to demonstrate that I wasn't the least bit affected by her negative mood. *Ignore difficult behaviour and it fades away.* Isn't that what the social worker on my last training course had assured us?

'Ow, that's *so* unfair,' she lamented, an aggressive growl taking the whine out of her voice. She leaned forward in her seat and flicked her forefinger close to the back of my head, almost making contact (another one of her habits whenever she grew tense). 'Today is literally the worst day of my life!'

Beside her, Reece began whining, his arms folded around his middle. 'Urgh, Rosie, I feel sick. I don't think I can go to school.'

'Oh, for God's sake!' Taylor bellowed before I could respond. 'Take no notice of 'im. He says it all the time so he can skive off school.'

Torn

'No I don't, you liar.'

'D'you want me to smash your head through that window?'

'Taylor,' I snapped, as a large 4 x 4 pulled out in front of me without indicating. I swung my Ford quickly to the left, taking the place it had vacated, and accidentally clipping the kerb with my offside wheel. The jolt nipped at the muscle I had torn in my shoulder when moving the beds around and I winced.

Taylor gasped and clutched her hands to her chest. 'Oh my God, oh my God, now I got whiplash!' She fluttered her hands around in front of her in a parody of shock. 'I can't believe you did that, Ro-sie-er!' she ejaculated, spitting my name out with such venom that it sounded like a swear word.

'Oh, Taylor, you'd make an excellent actress,' I said, trying to sound more amused than I felt. With only three days left of school before the Easter holidays, I knew I was going to have to find a way to establish a relationship with Taylor before they broke up. The withering glance she threw my way told me that I was going to have to be particularly inventive if I was to have any chance of achieving that.

As soon as I secured the handbrake Jamie dived forwards, kissed my cheek and leaped from the car. Thankfully, Emily offered to walk him to his classroom and as I watched them pass beneath the wrought-iron archway and into the playground, a pang of guilt rose in my chest because I wasn't there beside them. I had registered as a foster carer soon after separating from Gary, although I had been drawn to the idea ever since I discovered, at the age of thirteen, that my father had grown up in a children's home. A friend of mine, one of those scary people with a psychology degree, insisted that my attraction to fostering was born of a subconscious desire to heal my father and take away the pain he had felt as a child.

I wasn't sure about that, but on a practical level registering made sense – I needed to work but wanted to be available for Emily and Jamie whenever they needed me. Reality, as it often does, took me by surprise. In my head I had imagined that our future foster children would slot neatly into family life. Inevitably there would be problems, I knew that, but behavioural difficulties notwithstanding, we'd carry on pretty much as before. What I hadn't bargained on were the daily diaries, monthly reports, PEPs (personal education plans) meetings, LAC (looked-after child) reviews, health-care assessments, monthly visits from supervising and children's social workers, unannounced checks and, to top it all, providing transport to and from contact sessions with parents.

Not that I was complaining – my need to work with troubled children, like most foster carers, came deep from the heart and the children we had shared our home with over the last two years had done as much to help our family as we had ever done for them.

As I pulled away from the kerb, Taylor wincing exaggeratedly, I reminded myself that birth children learn lots of important life lessons from fostering, one being that simple, everyday comforts should never be taken for granted.

Without Jamie to chat to (the pair of them had barely stopped since they woke early that morning) Reece went into overdrive as we drove towards Downsedge Primary. My son, though lively, seemed to have a calming effect on Reece, but now he bounced up and down on his seat, talking so rapidly that I could barely keep up. 'How old do you think that BMW is then, Rosie?'

We had been playing the same game for ten minutes and I was getting a little jaded, but at least it seemed to be distracting him from his nervy, cramping stomach.

'Hmm, that's a tricky one because there aren't the usual letters and numbers on its registration plate,' I said, surveying his sister in the rear-view mirror as I spoke. She sat in stony silence, every so often releasing a faint scent of coconut as she tossed her blonde locks over her shoulder. Her hair really was a beautiful colour – burnished gold with flashes of red – and shiny from all the attention she seemed to lavish on it. I was surprised that she was wearing it loose to school but she had insisted that she was allowed to, although I was frankly disbelieving that the heavy liner she wore was permitted as well.

'Yes, but what do you *think*?'

'Well, the paintwork's shiny so I'd say two years old. Three at a push?'

Reece clapped a hand to his forehead as if something calamitous would happen as a direct result of my vagueness. 'Which one though? Two or three?'

My thoughts drifted back to the previous day when Reece had appeared anguished to be presented with a choice of beds. It seemed that he was a boy who preferred absolutes. 'Three, I'd say.'

He groaned, blinking rapidly to stop his eyes from twitching. As if contagious, one shoulder joined in, jerking up and down in synchrony with his eyelids. 'But how sure are you?'

'Quite, quite sure.'

Satisfied, his shoulders dropped in relief and I found myself letting out a breath as well. It was difficult not to get caught up in his panic.

'What about that van then? The Ford. How old do you think that is?'

Suppressing a sigh – he had chosen another vehicle with a personalised number plate – I hazarded a guess at five years. Reece chewed the ends of his nails as he considered my answer, his fingers visibly trembling. My heart went out to him; he seemed unable to cope with the tiniest amount of stress. Being so overwrought, it wasn't really any wonder that he suffered from so many tummy aches.

Suddenly his brow furrowed. 'What, so you're saying *that* van is more olderer than the BMW?' His alarmed tone suggested that my answer was outlandish and possibly downright dangerous.

'Well, it's just a guess, Reece, that's all. Why don't you tell me what you think? How old would you say it is?'

He seemed to know a lot about cars, surprising considering his age. With barely a glance he was able to identify the make and sometimes even the model of passing cars. I guessed that it must be a passion of his father's. It was a bad idea to throw the weight of responsibility back at him though, however knowledgeable he seemed. Clamping a hand either side of his head, he clawed at his nearly bare scalp with his fingers, an expression of pure panic skittering across his face.

'Owww, I don't know what to think. I really don't know.'

'Oh, for God's sake, shut it will yer, Reece? You're getting on my pissing nerves.'

I winced.

'You shut it,' Reece howled, his eyes pooling with tears. 'I'm trying to think. Ow, what shall I guess? I really don't know, Rosie.'

'It don't bloody matter how old it is-er,' Taylor snapped.

Not entirely unsympathetic with the sentiment, I said: 'Please don't say "shut it", both of you. Say "be quiet" instead. And mind your language, Taylor.'

She rolled her eyes. 'Well, bloody be quiet then, Reece, or I'll knock your teeth to the back of your throat.'

'Erm, how about we count how many vans we see from here until we reach school?' I ventured, knowing that Jamie adored nothing more than being presented with a challenge. He really wasn't that much older than Reece. Besides, distraction was top of the list of social workers' tips for dealing with difficult behaviour.

'OK! You do it as well, Rosie, yeah?'

Performing a mental punch in the air, I tried not to whoop. 'Absolutely, but we'll have to be quiet so I can concentrate.'

Reece pinched his forefinger and thumb together and mimed zipping his lips together, a sight that brought a little skip to my heart. Taylor rolled her eyes and stared avidly out of the window, her forehead almost touching the glass. Downsedge Primary was about six miles on from Emily and Jamie's school and it was already nearing 9 o'clock. Traffic grew mercifully lighter as we reached the outskirts of town, the wider, tree-lined streets windswept from the previous day's storm.

At 9.15 a.m. we finally pulled up outside Downsedge Primary, the school's appearance incongruous with its earthy name. Topped with several spired turrets, the four-storey red-brick building reminded me of my own primary school, its many cottage pane windows dotted with colourful paintings and glittered mobiles. 'S'ya later,' Taylor said, throwing her school bag over her shoulder and striding off without a backward glance.

'Have a lovely day,' I called out to her back as I got out of the car and handed a book bag to Reece.

He sniffed, his big eyes pricking with tears. 'I don't wanna go to school,' he cried mournfully. 'I want Mummy.'

'Aw, come here, love,' I said softly, holding out my arms. He rushed forwards and buried his head into my chest.

Sometimes it was that easy.

Later that afternoon, I decided to head off any negativity over my cooking skills by inviting Taylor to help me in the kitchen. Sitting on the sofa watching television, she seemed taken aback by the offer, staring between me and the screen as if she couldn't quite believe what she was hearing. 'What, me?' she said, thumbing herself in the chest.

I laughed. 'Yes, but you don't have to. It's up to you.'

'All right,' she said, which, in Taylor's personal vocabulary constituted enthusiastic acceptance. She shuffled towards the kitchen with slow wariness, as if suspicious that the floor space between the living room and kitchen might be set with a series of small mines.

'Turn the TV off on your way through, could you?' I said, standing in the doorway that separated the kitchen from the living room, wiping my hands on a paper kitchen towel.

'I want it on.'

'Well, no one else is watching it and we'll be quite a while. I thought we could have lasagne today, although we'll make Reece a small one without onions.'

'Na. I like it on in the background.'

'But what about our environmental footprint?' I said, trying to sound jokey. Since arriving home from school she had spent over half an hour on the computer, assuring me that she never ever went anywhere near chatrooms ('I swear on my life, Rosie, for God's sake-er!'), and the rest of the time watching Disney sitcoms that seemed more suited to teenagers than someone of her age. But at least they were milder than *CSI*, a television programme she insisted her parents allowed her to watch. I reached for the remote and switched it off. 'Now, how confident are you with a sharp knife? Have you used one before?'

Taylor was too savvy to be sidetracked. Drawing herself to her full height (roughly an inch shorter than me) she set her jaw and flicked her fingers close to my eye. I stood unmoving, not wanting to give her the satisfaction of flinching away. 'Changed me mind, I don't wanna help you now. Put it back on, can yer? I wanna finish me programme.'

I hesitated, trying to work out whether agreeing would make me seem like too much of a pushover. Whenever Taylor refused to do something I was instantly ruffled, a sad indictment of my lack of experience. It was so much easier with toddlers, I thought. Counting to five and then sweeping them up in my arms if they refused to co-operate. Flailing, pudgy limbs and tiny fists were well within my capabilities. And then I reminded myself that I was supposed to be the adult so, unwilling to get drawn into childish games, I said: 'Well, OK, but it's going off in an hour when dinner's ready.'

Just over an hour later I asked everyone to wash their hands. Six plates were arranged on trays I had bought earlier, since there was no longer a dining table for us to sit around. Taylor didn't move.

'Taylor, could you turn the television off and wash your hands for dinner, please?'

'Just give us my tray here, ta,' she said blithely from the sofa, as if she had special dispensation from the rules that the rest of us followed. When I hesitated she flicked her wrist at me as if to say, 'Come on, come on'.

I drew a deep breath and walked backwards from the kitchen to the living room. 'I'd like you to wash your hands like everyone else, please, Taylor.'

Teeth bared, she threw me a disgusted look and then slowly dragged herself to her feet, groaning as if crippled with arthritis. When she returned from the bathroom the television was off and all of us were sitting down, trays on our laps. It wasn't ideal but when the weather improved I planned to scrub the patio table and chairs down so that we could eat our meals outside.

Instead of taking the space on the sofa that I'd left for her, Taylor reached over me to grab the remote.

Reece stiffened, the muscles in his cheeks tensing so hard that I could see them trembling.

'It's all right, Reece,' I said gently. 'There's nothing to worry about, but, Taylor, we're not having the television on while we eat. Now, sit down, please, there's a love.'

She threw her arms up in disbelief. 'Oh, why not-er?' she screeched. 'Mum lets us have it on all the time.'

Well, Mum's not here is she? I was tempted to say. But I didn't. Instead, I took a breath and then overwrote the mental retort: 'Everyone has different rules, Taylor. In our house we each get to choose some programmes we'd like to watch. You and Reece can as well, but the TV doesn't stay on all the time. You've been on the computer and watched some TV. I think that's enough screen time for the moment. Now, come on, sit down or your dinner will get cold.'

Torn between eating and flouncing off, she stood for a moment, rocking on her heels. Food won out in the end. Without further demur, she slumped herself down on the sofa, so hard that Emily's plate flew up, some pasta sliding onto her lap. She stared at Taylor with an expression of forbearance, glanced at me then silently lifted her knees, cradling the tray closer to her lap. I felt a flare of gratitude for her Zen-like nature, her ability to take upsets in her stride.

'So, how was school today, guys?'

Reece spoke through a visible roux of pasta and mince. 'Mrs Stanley moved me up to green level for my reading,' he mumbled, tomato sauce dripping from the side of his mouth. I resisted the urge to say anything about it; they had only arrived twenty-four hours earlier and there was so much for them to take in. Table manners were lower down my list of priorities than making them feel comfortable and I didn't want to be constantly nagging them.

'Well done, Reece. That sounds good,' I said, clueless as to what green level meant. Emily and Jamie had worked their way up a numbered reading scheme at their school.

'It ain't good,' he said, shovelling an overburdened forkful in his mouth. 'Still way too easy for me. The stories are boring.'

'Oh, well, perhaps we could have a word with your teacher about that.'

He nodded, looking pleased.

'Bethany's still on those green books,' Taylor piped up, suddenly emerging from her sulk.

'Who's Bethany?' I asked, keen to encourage a continuing thaw.

'Oh, just some lame girl in my class.'

'What's lame about her?'

'Everything, basically.'

I lowered my fork to the tray. 'Everyone has something special about them, Taylor. Perhaps you should give this Bethany a break.'

She sighed heavily, eyes skyward. 'God, I don't think so. For a start she wears glasses, no offence, Reece.'

Reece narrowed his eyes and looked at me as if undecided whether he should feel insulted or not. 'So does Harry Potter,' I said, winking at him. That was all it took. His face lit up and he carried on eating.

'Yeah, well, Bethany's fat as well. Oh, the other day it was hilarious, yeah? You shoulda been there. Basically, we was in the hall for games, right? Cos the field's blocked off at the moment with all scaffolding and stuff. And she goes and falls over and literally skids all the way across the floor on her arse.' I looked up from my plate but she carried on, oblivious. 'Oh my God, it was so fucking funny. And she always has these marks on her arms where her uniform clings to her. We call her Lardface.'

'Please don't use bad language in front of the others, Taylor. If you must say something, say, "Oh my giddy aunt" or how about, "Oh my goodness"?'

Her jaw dropped. 'You have *got* to be kidding? What bad language anyway?'

I pressed my lips together and gave her a hard stare. She rolled her eyes. 'Oh what's the big deal? Everyone swears.'

I gave her another warning glare but she seemed guileless. Second nature to her, I don't think she even realised she was doing it. 'Poor Bethany, it must be so horrible for her, being called names,' I said. 'I bet she dreads going to school.'

A faint shadow of embarrassment crossed Taylor's features, quickly followed by a 'Who cares?' shrug. 'It ain't just me. Literally everyone hates her.'

I winced. 'Hate is a very strong word, love.'

'I'm a strong person,' she said with a sour smile. She always seemed to have an answer for everything.

We lapsed into silence, none of us quite sure how to restart the conversation. And then Emily, who had been quiet until that point, said: 'I hope Bethany discovers a cure for cancer or something when she's older, don't you, Mum?'

I was about to agree when Taylor scoffed. 'It'd be just like her to do something lame.'

Jamie dropped his fork. It clattered on the tray and made Emily jump again. Her plate rolled against her tummy, tomato sauce creeping over her top. 'How can finding a cure for cancer be lame?' Jamie demanded, looking at me with wide eyes. Emily glanced between us, gave her top a little shake and then discreetly shuffled her bottom further along the sofa, away from Taylor. Her ability to accept the bad in people without too much effort always amazed me, whereas Jamie was the opposite. Even at the age of seven he couldn't tolerate flippant, senseless remarks.

'Because I say it is, numbskull.' Taylor flicked her hair over her shoulder. 'Basically I'm gonna be a top model or something when I'm fourteen. I could of been one already if it weren't for school and everything.'

Jamie spluttered on his food, his eyes scrunched in disbelief. Sensing that he was about to make a comment that wouldn't go down too well I jumped in quickly. 'Some of the most famous people in the world were picked on at school, did you know that?'

'Yeah, like who?' Taylor asked, her lip curled into a grimace. I knew it didn't matter what I said, but I pushed ahead anyway, if only to distract Jamie.

'Er, well, off the top of my head, there's Madonna. She had a hard time at school.'

Taylor rolled her eyes. 'Lame,' she decreed.

'Lame? You're calling Madonna lame?'

'Yep,' she said, rolling her lips and making a loud smacking sound. I ran through a host of other celebrities, reaching a point where I had no idea whether they were bullied or not. Taylor wrote them all off as boring losers, or useless twats. Riled, Jamie shouted 'Richer than you'll ever be' after each of her insults.

It saddened me that a child of her age should be so disillusioned with the world that every word she uttered seemed to be either a put-down or a complaint. I knew that most children had a tendency to polarise, dividing experiences or people into the best or the worst ever, but Taylor categorised almost everything in existence as abominable. The only person she ever spoke well of was her mother, who was, in Taylor's words, 'beautiful and kind'.

It puzzled me, her adoration of her mother, considering that she seemed to be the prime aggressor towards the children.

Chapter Five

Two days later, on the last day of term, the doorbell rang barely ten minutes after I'd arrived home from the school run. It had been a difficult forty-eight hours and so, even though there wasn't a single line through any of the chores on my 'to-do' list and it was my last chance to get everything done without all the children at home, I could have hugged the weighty woman standing on the doorstep when I noticed the official-looking identity card hanging around her neck.

'Karron, Bright Heights,' she said in a heavy American accent. 'You weren't expecting me, right?'

Since Taylor and Reece's arrival I hadn't heard anything from social services and there were so many questions I wanted to ask, so much I felt I needed to get off my chest. As Karron was from my fostering agency she wouldn't have direct information on the children; that would come from Maisie. Even so, it was a relief to see someone official.

'Er, no I wasn't but I – it's very good to see you,' I said, pulling off a pair of pink rubber gloves. 'Please, come in.' My usual supervising social worker from the fostering agency was on a sabbatical from social work and Bright Heights hadn't told me who was filling in for him. A TV and film extra in his younger days, Des had left two months earlier for California, where he'd managed to secure a bit part in a hospital drama for a cable network. We had developed quite a close friendship since meeting two years earlier and besides being sorry to see him go, I was anxious about who might replace him. The backbone of fostering, early on in a placement, is often a daily grind of stress – an effective supervising social worker can transform the way a foster carer deals with those early problems, often just by offering unswerving support.

'We'll record this as one of your unannounced then,' said Karron as she shrugged off her denim jacket and draped it over the side table in the hall. Social workers are required to make a minimum of two unannounced visits to the foster home each year to check that standards of care are being maintained and all is as it should be. So far I'd been lucky – they had failed to catch me in on those days when the house was covered in a fine layer of dust, Lego strewn across the floor.

'This is my son, Jamie,' I said as Karron followed me through the living room. Jamie was tucked up on the sofa, immersed in reading a book. 'He's feeling a bit poorly today.'

'Well, hi there, Jamie,' Karron chirped. 'Nothing too bad I hope.'

Jamie had slept badly, his asthma, which was normally fairly well-controlled, flaring up at the onset of a cold. Now, though, he was looking perkier than he had for hours. I guessed that Karron's accent – one he usually only heard on TV – had brought on the sudden improvement. 'I'm a bit wheezy,' he said, grinning from ear to ear.

'Ah, poor guy. You rest up. I'll talk to your mom in the kitchen.'

Jamie nodded, watching her with amused interest.

As I filled the kettle, Karron dropped her bag on the kitchen floor then leaned slantwise on the worktop, elbows down, chin resting on one fist. Her hair was wavy, brown and long, reaching halfway down her back. At a guess, I put her in her mid-40s, though the shiny lipstick and sparkling eye shadow she wore gave her a youthful air. With the top half of her chest strewn over the wooden chopping board and her legs stretched out behind her, she looked thoroughly at home. The sight immediately lowered my guard so that when we'd finished making small talk and she asked how things were going, I felt I could tell her anything.

'Difficult,' I said, reaching for two mugs from the top cupboard. I lowered them to the worktop and turned to face her. 'Reece is settling well I think. He's very jumpy, craves security, but he's turning to me for comfort so I'm not *too* worried about him. He's very sweet. I had a word with his teacher this morning about his reading books. He wanted to move on to something a bit more challenging and when she agreed he was over the moon, bless him.

Taylor though –' I paused, lifting two jars of coffee up for Karron to choose from. She gestured towards the smallest with a nod of her head. 'Black and strong,' she said, 'and don't hold back on the sugar.'

I grinned, already certain that Karron was going to be a rock.

'What about Taylor?' she asked, helping herself to one of the biscuits on a plate in front of her. 'She's ten, right?'

'Yep, ten. Going on fifteen.' I scooped two generous teaspoons of instant coffee into one of the mugs and a teabag into the other. 'I think we may have got off on the wrong foot,' I said, narrowing my eyes against the rising steam as I poured hot water from the kettle into the mugs. Karron took the proffered drink and listened without interrupting as I explained the mix-up over their sex. 'As soon as I laid eyes on them I thought they wouldn't be able to stay and so I'm afraid I didn't give them the welcome they deserved.'

Karron sipped cautiously at her coffee, leaving a trace of coral lipstick on the rim. 'But you sorted things, right?'

'Well, yes, with moving the rooms around and everything,' I called out as I pottered to the fridge, removing the milk. 'Oh, I don't know, maybe it's nothing to do with that, but Taylor seems so angry. With me mostly,' I added, pouring some milk into my tea.

After returning the carton to the fridge I sat on a stool at the breakfast bar and waited for Karron to respond.

She tilted her head to one side, eyeing me with a bright, intuitive gaze. 'She's gonna be though, isn't she? I mean, that's a normal response, right?'

'Absolutely, yes, of course it is. But –' Suddenly lost for words, I glanced into the garden. The March sun hung low over our tumble-down fence, our border of daffodils iridescent under the cloudless sky. A single yellow petal, browning at the edges, was torn off by the breeze and danced a wild jig across the lawn. Behind me, the fridge hummed, loud and rattling, as if egging me on to say something. I sighed, wondering how to put my feelings of helplessness into words.

'But?' prompted Karron.

With a teaspoon still clasped in my fingers, I lifted my hands. 'I know it sounds silly. Of course she's going to be angry. And hurt and confused and lost – I know all of that and I understand. I do.' I sighed, looking Karron in the eye. 'I suppose the real problem is –' I hesitated, took a breath. It was a tough one to articulate, because somehow I felt that as a foster carer, I should know better. 'Well, I suppose the truth is that I really don't know how to deal with her.' I placed the teaspoon firmly on the side. 'There, I've said it now.'

'Feels good, huh?' Karron was watching me with a slight, knowing smile on her face.

'To let it out?' I nodded. 'Yes I suppose it does.'

She took another sip of her coffee, cradled the cup in her hands and then lifted her elbows towards me. 'You know, you mustn't beat up on yourself for having doubts; the best foster carers are the ones that question themselves. Those who think they're perfect are the ones I worry about. So – go for it, girl. Gimme me all you got.'

'OK, you asked for it,' I said with a wry smile. 'Well, for a start she sneers at everything I say. I mean literally, every time I open my mouth. If I ask her to stop doing something all she comes back with is: "Why should I?" Oh and she does this infuriating thing,' I said, flicking my fingers close to my eyes. 'It's SO annoying! She falls short of making contact so when I ask her to stop she says: "God-er, I never even touched you! You're sooooo moody." She's obsessed with the computer, some site called Myspace in particular, and she goes nuts when I tell her that she's had enough screen time. There's just –'

I stopped, noticing that Karron was staring at me with a dubious expression. 'Myspace? I don't think she should be on there. Myspace has an age rating, I believe.'

'Taylor told me that it's a kids' site. She said all of her friends are on there.'

Karron stifled a snigger and I reddened, covering my face with my hands. What a fool I was, being so easily duped. 'Don't worry about it,' the social worker said as I slowly lowered them. 'They all try it on. Check it out but I'm pretty sure you have to be around thirteen or fourteen.'

I sighed. Disagreements over screen time were nothing new – even Emily and Jamie baulked sometimes when I asked them to turn their gadgets off, and they had grown up with the same, consistent rules. Children who had been given free rein online were bound to find the sudden imposition of restrictions frustrating, I knew that, and clashes over screen time were common in foster carers' homes. 'They'll be no reasoning with her if she's not allowed to use it. It's like you can almost feel an undercurrent of aggression whenever she walks into the room, slamming the door behind her. I know it's only been four days and I sound like such a lightweight but, really, the thought of having her around all day for the next two weeks –' I tapped the worktop with my fingers, my mind so caught up in the events of the last few days that I was looking at Karron without really registering her. 'It's a bit daunting to be honest. She won't even get ready for school in the morning. And then once she's there, she won't come home.'

Karron knitted her brow. 'Huh?'

'Sit-ins. She performs sit-ins, refusing to leave her classroom. It was 5 o'clock before she agreed to come home yesterday afternoon. Thankfully my ex-husband had collected Emily and Jamie or they'd have been waiting for me at the school gates. I've a nasty feeling she's going to do it again this afternoon and what with Jamie feeling under the weather and all my back-up carers busy,' I took a breath, 'well, I'm out of ideas. I just don't know what to do about it.'

'What does the school say?'

'Taylor's teacher is as exasperated as I am,' I said with a rueful smile. 'She's only young and it's playing havoc with her social life.'

Karron broke into infectious laughter.

I grinned. 'It sounds funny but at the time it's so frustrating. And do you know the really odd thing?'

The social worker tilted her head.

'I get the feeling that her heart isn't in it at all. There's no denying that she's a big personality. She's bullish and dynamic, and she's got a mighty temper. But there are times when I think she's acting up because she thinks she should.' I rubbed my hand over my hair. 'I don't know, maybe I'm wrong, but sometimes I get the feeling she finds it all as tiresome as I do. It's as if she's stuck playing a role and there's nothing anyone can do to help.'

There was a pause, Karron examining her plump hands as if searching for an answer among the network of veins. 'I'm tempted to tell you to grab her hand and drag her out but, heck, you'd get into a whole heap of trouble if you did that. You Brits are just so uptight.'

I laughed out loud. 'You're right there. So, what *can* I do?'

Karron lifted her hands, palms upward. 'When it comes to kids, there's one universal truth: they think the world revolves around them. I swear to God, I've known the most stubborn kids willing to move mountains for a few extra dollars in their pocket money. That's the only thing I can think of – tempting her away with something she badly wants. Have you spoken to her social worker about it?'

'Maisie? Yes, I called her yesterday but she wasn't – well, she's a bit – she wasn't much help, to be honest.'

'A bit what?'

I chewed my lip. 'Erm, a bit, you know ...'

The social worker shook her head.

'A bit airy-fairy.'

Karron slapped her hand down on the worktop. 'Airy-fairy?! W-hat the hell does that mean?'

'Um. A bit too far left of liberal. You know what I mean don't you? Away with the fairies.'

She was still looking bemused. 'You mean she's crap at her job?'

My jaw dropped. 'No, no, I'm not saying that at all. I'm sure she's very nice. I don't know her that well anyway and –'

'Jeeez, you lot are hard work,' said Karron, shaking her head and laughing. 'You're all just so polite. I love England, don't get me wrong, but sometimes you just gotta let go, you know?'

Behind Karron, I could see Jamie craning his head, trying to keep track of our conversation.

I nodded, suppressing a grin.

'In the States we're not afraid to use commands. Sure, we call them instructions, but that's just splitting hairs. It's all the same damn thing. We're a lot tougher on parents too, back home. If we remove a child, the parents have a year to get themselves together or they're out of the picture. And they have to do it of their own free will; we don't have all the help and programmes you have here. The Brits treat everyone with kid gloves, but sometimes folks just need telling, you know? So they know what's expected. If they fall short, well, that's their own damn fault. You can be as polite as you wanna be but kids need to understand that your requests ain't optional.'

'I have tried that, Karron. I can be firm when I want to be.'

She raised her eyebrows as if she found that idea difficult to imagine.

'I can, really. But when you're dealing with someone who doesn't seem to give a hoot, the usual rules fly out of the window. In terms of discipline, my hands are tied – I can't limit her pocket money or send her to her room. What can I do?'

Karron frowned. 'Hmm, I've got a feeling that there's a refresher course coming up with all the latest techniques for managing difficult behaviour. I'll give them a call and book you in, that OK?'

I nodded, feeling lighter somehow. When social workers are judgemental, foster carers clam up and, in the end, everyone suffers. It was refreshing to be able to sit with a professional and talk in a leisured, conversational way about the problems I was experiencing. 'Great,' said Karron, lowering her empty mug to the worktop. Then, as she gathered up her diary and handbag, she asked something that secured her position as one of the best social workers I had ever known, aside from Des. 'So, how are your two coping with all of this?'

I took a breath. 'Fairly well. I mean, Jamie and Reece hit it off straight away; it's like they're already best buddies. And over the last day or two Emily and Taylor have been spending more time together. They both love art so they've been colouring and making beaded bracelets.'

Karron tilted her head. 'But?'

I took a breath, raised my eyes to the ceiling. 'Taylor and Jamie,' I sliced my hand through the air, whispering so that Jamie couldn't hear. 'Not so good. Every time Jamie speaks

Taylor rolls her eyes or makes some comment. It's difficult to watch.'

Karron nodded, bit her lip. 'I'll get you booked onto that course. You might find it helps a bit, though sometimes it's just a case of gritting your teeth and getting through the ugly bit.'

I gave her a grim smile and she patted my arm. 'Right, if that's all,' she turned to walk away and then spun around. 'Oh, wait up, I've gotta tell you, there's been a complaint.'

I grimaced, wondering why she hadn't mentioned it before. 'Oh no! What?'

'Take it easy, Rosie. It's no big deal. The older one, what's her name again?'

'Taylor?'

'Yeah, right. She's told her mum that she's not allowed to watch TV.'

I blew out a frustrated lungful of air. 'That's not true! All I said was we're not leaving it on all the time.'

'Fair enough,' Karron shrugged. 'Anyway, Mum's complained to the local authority and the social worker, Millie, did you say?'

I shook my head. 'Maisie.'

Karron poked the air with her forefinger. 'Yep. She got on to me. Asked me to offer you some words of advice.'

I pressed my lips together. 'So what now?'

Karron shrugged. 'If she complains again, tell her to read a book. And take that worried look off your face! You're doing just fine.'

As she walked through the living room she lifted her hand towards Jamie. He waved back, watching her avidly. 'You take care, little guy. I'll be seeing y'all soon.'

She was gone by the time the thought occurred to me – when did Taylor get a chance to speak to her mum?

Back in the living room, Jamie looked appalled. 'She's been complaining about us,' he said, his eyes glistening with angry tears.

'Not *us* exactly,' I said, mildly, perching on the edge of the sofa beside him. 'She's just upset about having to leave her parents and she's looking for ways to let all the bad stuff out.' I stroked his fringe back from his forehead. 'It's scary, coming into foster care.'

Absorbing what I'd said, his eyes flickered and then his expression softened. 'Yeah, I suppose, but –' he gave me a sideways glance then looked away, picking at the bobbles on the blanket covering his knees, '– I don't really like her much. Taylor.' After a moment he looked up, assessing my reaction.

I grabbed his hand. 'I know it's been difficult, honey, but things will improve.' As I spoke, I was aware of the lack of conviction in my own voice.

'How long's she staying?'

'I have no idea yet,' I said, guilt tightening my chest so that my voice sounded strained. I cleared my throat. 'But we'll do lots of nice things over the next two weeks, OK? I'm sure that will help everything to settle. By the time you go back to school you'll be feeling differently, you just wait and see.'

Still at the age when parents seemed to know everything, he brightened, wrapping his arms around my neck for a hug. 'So, what did you think of our new supervising social worker?' I asked, pulling back.

'She's so cool!' he said. 'Why does she talk like that?'

'She's American.'

His eyes widened. 'Des is in America. Do you think she's met him?'

I smiled, giving his cheek an affectionate pinch. 'I doubt it. America is a huge country.'

He frowned, concentrating. 'Which part of America is she from? Near Disneyland?'

'You mean, which *state*. Hmm, I'm not sure. Sounds to me as if she's from the South. I'll ask her next time, if you like.'

Jamie slapped his knee. 'Sure thang, Mom!'

I laughed absent-mindedly, my thoughts drifting back to the mystery contact between Taylor and her mum. Apart from going to school, Taylor hadn't been out of my sight since the day she had arrived. How on earth had she got a message to her mum?

Chapter Six

Five o'clock came and went, and then five-thirty, but still Taylor wouldn't budge. Sitting on one of the desks with her legs dangling ungainly over the side, she had assumed her default *couldn't care less* pose, her every pore emitting the insouciant message that however much I reasoned or even begged, she was not going to be moved. Hovering at the brink of losing my patience, I moved across the room, distancing myself from her.

Through the open window I took a few deep breaths and watched a lone cleaner sweeping the deserted playground, clearing away the detritus of the school day. Jamie, his chest still whistling slightly but with much more colour in his cheeks, leaned against the wall at the far end of the year six classroom, legs crossed in front of him. With a puzzle on the rug between them, Reece lay on his side opposite Jamie, head propped on his elbow and legs twitching in that restless, nervous way of his.

'What's the time *now*, Rosie?' Reece whined, strumming two fingers on his chunky thigh.

'Four minutes later than when you last asked,' I said with an apologetic glance towards Miss Cooper, Taylor's class teacher. It was well past her clocking off time but she kindly waved my apologies away. Every now and again Jamie dropped his head back against the wall and closed his eyes, exhausted after his sleepless night. As he did so, fresh bubbles of irritation rose in my chest. I had planned to prepare an early dinner so that he could get to bed and rest but there was small chance of that now. The secretary at Emily's school had helpfully added her to the after-school chess club, even though, strictly speaking, it was full. The club ended at 6 o'clock and after that, I simply didn't know what I would do. Of all the juggling required of a busy mum, I always found that the logistical challenge of having to be in two places at once was one of the most stressful. As each minute passed, I felt the pressure building.

Needless to say, Taylor was showing no sign of weakness. Sliding from the desk, she flopped into a chair and rested her elbows on the desk in front of her, head propped in her upturned hands. What gives you the right to hold all of us to ransom like this? I thought, quietly seething. But then, as I watched her sigh lazily, I got the sense that she was play acting again. Stretching out her legs, it was as if she was working hard to give the impression that she was set to stay for the next few hours. And yet, her momentary pained expression told a different story.

Trying my hardest to appear untouched by her antics, I paced the classroom and pretended to study text messages on my mobile phone, clinging onto the faint hope that if I refused to play my part in the stand-off, she might get bored and surrender. I had already left two messages with Maisie and was hoping she hadn't already left the office for the day.

A few minutes later, Taylor stretched her arms above her head and shuffled around on her chair. I held my breath, willing her to give in. I could hardly believe it when, with a backward scrape of her chair, she leaned her hands flat on the desk and made to move. The boys scrambled to their feet. 'Oh, finally,' Jamie huffed, noisily blowing air from his cheeks. Taylor hesitated in a half-crouch and then sank back down, arms folded tightly across her chest.

A disjointed moment followed, none of us quite sure what had passed. When it became clear that she was in for the long haul, my heart sank.

'Oh no-o-o –' Jamie groaned, looking at me in mute appeal. It was as if he couldn't quite believe my powerlessness, my inability to take control.

Edging close to losing it I closed my eyes, summoning every last vestige of serenity I could muster. Behaving badly is an effective way of finding out whether she's safe, I told myself, remembering something I'd learned in training. When children were testing their limits, it often helped to see past the behaviour and think about the cause instead. Unfortunately, even that wasn't really helping. Generally I considered myself a patient person but Taylor's stubbornness really went beyond the pale. What I found most irritating was her total control and our utter helplessness. She knew there was nothing we could do to make her move and I feared the power would go to her head so that she would become even more difficult to handle.

'Taylor,' Miss Cooper said pleadingly, with a note of desperation in her voice. The ten-year-old, chewing her cheeks as if rolling a piece of gum around her mouth, lifted her head and looked at her teacher nonchalantly.

'We're all getting very tired now. I really think it's time we stopped this, don't you, darling?'

Taylor gave a derisory snort and ran her fingers through her hair, the golden tresses glinting amber in the low afternoon sun. Personally I felt the endearment was over-generous and I was also pretty certain that appealing to her better nature simply wasn't going to work.

I walked over to the window again, my phone vibrating in the pocket of my jeans. I pulled it out, half-aware of Miss Cooper's continued cajoling. It was Maisie. I breathed a sigh of relief and then, in hushed tones, filled her in.

'Oh dear,' she said in low, sluggish tone. 'I know she was unhappy about the sit-u-a-tion with the TV. Did your supervising social worker speak to you about that?'

My stomach contracted. 'Yes, she mentioned it,' I said slowly. 'But I don't think it's that at all.'

'Have you resolved the issue then? I made the sug-gestion that you buy a portable and leave it on somewhere in the house.'

'Oh right. No, Karron didn't say anything about that.' I felt a flare of gratitude to Karron for dismissing the idea without even troubling me. Forcing myself to fight my own corner, I took a breath (that's another thing they don't mention when you register as a foster carer – if you dislike confrontation, you'd better get over it, and quickly.) 'To be honest, Maisie, I don't like that idea,' I said, trying to keep a congenial tone. 'Taylor gets to watch quite a bit of TV and it really isn't anything we can't negotiate between us. What concerns me more is how she spoke to her mum without me knowing. There's been no contact between them as far as I know.'

'Ah yes, I meant to talk to you about that. Taylor has her own mobile but her calls should be lim-i-ted to twice a week and arranged for a particular time of day. You are aware, I presume, that foster carers are supposed to super-vise all contact with parents when they're at home?'

'I had no idea she even had a phone,' I said in hushed tones, running my fingers through my hair. I paced the length of the window and back again, trying to keep my cool. 'Now I'm aware, of course I'll be supervising the calls.'

One of the difficulties inherent in fostering is that so many everyday issues lie outside of the foster carers' control. It is natural for children to test their limits, to rail against the boundaries set for them and those in care often play their foster carers off against social workers. It was in Taylor's best interests for the adults taking care of her to form a united front, but unfortunately that seemed unlikely in this case.

Maisie's tone softened a little. 'Good, thank you. I'm trying to organise a contact session for tomorrow so that the children can see their parents. Nick and Claire have been told that they'll have to complete a parenting course before the children are returned, but they're resisting that at the moment. We're thinking two contacts a week initially, on Tuesdays and Fridays, so phone calls home should be scheduled for Mondays and Thursdays, that way the children's weekends are free. I haven't got a concrete time yet so I'll give you a call in the morning if that's OK?'

'Yes, fine.'

'So, I hope things resolve themselves quickly.'

I gave a short laugh. 'Hmm, well, she'll move when she gets hungry enough I suppose.'

There was a short pause. 'Oh, has she not eaten?' Maisie asked, sounding concerned.

'No, I told you. She's not moved from her desk since the bell went at three-fifteen.'

Another silence and then Maisie said: 'Oh, that's not good.' She then went on to suggest, in all seriousness, that I aid and abet the sit-in by offering Taylor some refreshments in case she became dehydrated. Lost for words, I merely snorted.

'The local authority will come under fire if one of their carers withholds food and drink from a child,' Maisie droned, her tone frosting over again.

I was silent, overwhelmed by a sudden anger. In the background I could hear a door slamming and people talking. It sounded as if Maisie was walking down a corridor, probably leaving the office for the day. *You come and sit here and wait for her to move then*, I wanted to bite back. Her lack of support was galling.

'Offer plenty of positive praise when she does show willing to come home,' she continued over a loud clunk, presumably the closing of a car door and a rumble as she turned the ignition of her car. I pictured an embroidered bag full of empty Red Bull cans on the front passenger seat and Maisie behind the wheel, eager to end the call so that she could head off to the comfort of home.

After shoving the handset back into my pocket I stared out of the window, trying to gather some composure. It wasn't easy, with Maisie's disapproving tone reverberating in my ears and Taylor's eyes fixed on my back.

'Who was that?' the ten-year-old demanded a few moments later.

I half-turned and opened my mouth to speak but then stilled, thinking.

'Well, who was it?'

Slowly, I turned around. The words that came out of my mouth floated from the past, a well-worn phrase used by my mother when I was a child and one I had never repeated, until now. 'Never you mind.'

She glowered. 'It was Maisie, weren't it?'

'It may have been,' I said vaguely, in a deliberate show of nonchalance. I strolled back to the window, linked my hands behind my back and pretended to study the newly swept playground.

'What did she say?'

'I'd rather not go into it, Taylor,' I said calmly, keeping my back towards her.

Sensing an ensuing battle, Reece sat up sharply, his head darting back and forth between us as if watching a tennis match. Twitching, his eyes crumpled and he jabbed his fists into them, trying to rub it away.

'You gotta tell me,' she said, bestowing me with a violent stare. 'I wanna know how my mum is. And Bailey. And Jimmy.'

The 'when and then' technique suddenly floated into my mind, something else I had learnt in training. I turned around to face her and levelled my gaze. '*When* you're ready to come home, *then* I'll tell you all about it.'

'It ain't my home,' she retorted, but scraped her chair back noisily and got to her feet. I stiffened, hardly daring to hope that it had worked. Miss Cooper's jaw tensed, her hands clenched into fists.

'Yes!' Jamie cheered as Taylor reached for her rucksack and sloped off towards the door. I closed my eyes, savouring the blissful moment of relief. Reece charged after Taylor and Jamie, pale with tiredness, rested his head on my upper arm. Miss Cooper and I exchanged a significant glance as we followed the siblings along the empty corridor, our footsteps echoing off the walls. We were both uncomfortably aware, I think, that in two weeks' time, after the Easter holidays, we were likely to go through the whole experience all over again.

Chapter Seven

As soon as Taylor secured her seatbelt I thanked her for co-operating (delivering the positive praise without a trace of the resentment swirling around my chest) and then relayed the information Maisie had given me about contact. Reece cheered on hearing the news but Taylor seemed to withdraw into herself, staring moodily out of the window. Knowing how desperate she was to see her mum, her muted reaction struck me as strange.

'Rosi-e-e,' Reece said. My heart sank. The number-plate game might just have been enough to tip me over the edge. 'If someone offered you five hundred thousand million pounds to have a stinky name like Poo Poo would you do it?'

Jamie giggled, his breath catching as his chest rumbled in a loud wheeze. I smiled, brightening. This struck me as an easier game and one unlikely to result in unnecessary stress. 'Erm, yes probably.'

'Urgh, Mom!' Jamie shrieked as if I'd actually agreed to change my name by deed poll. Since Karron's visit, he had taken to calling me Mom instead of Mum, the rascal, squeezing in Americanisms wherever he could. He and Reece were staring at each other, mouths stretched open in shocked hilarity.

'Would you do it for two hundred million pounds?'

'Yep,' I said definitely, enjoying their disgust.

'One hundred million?'

'Absolutely.'

'How about half a million?'

'Of course I would.'

'A quarter of a million?'

I hesitated for a moment, to give the impression I was giving the matter my most serious consideration. 'Erm, I don't think so, no.'

In the rear-view mirror I could see the boys looking at each other. Jamie was smiling but Reece's forehead had crumpled. Oh no, I thought, here we go. 'So you wouldn't do it for anything less than half a million?'

'No I wouldn't,' I said with a nod of my head, guessing that a definite answer was what he would be most comfort-able with.

He was quiet for a second or two and I began to relax, but then he made an anxious noise in his throat. 'So you're saying if someone offered you *one* pound less you wouldn't do it?'

I paused. 'Nope, definitely not.'

He slapped his forehead and ran his fingers over and

over his hair. 'You're saying you wouldn't do it, not even for just one pound different?'

'Nope.'

'That's crazy!' He and Jamie carolled, shaking their heads. Since Karron's visit, it had been another one of Jamie's catchphrases, one that Reece had adopted as his own. Jamie laughed again but Reece bumped his head in anguish, once, twice, three times against the glass.

About half a mile from Emily's school, Taylor began kicking the back of my seat – a gentle nudge rather than an outright assault and so I quickly decided to ignore it – but, like the soft thrum of a dripping tap, it was the sort of low-level irritation that held the potential of driving a person to distraction. I knew that simply asking her to stop wouldn't work and was likely to escalate the situation, so, with a ferocious grip on the steering wheel, I tried to drown out Reece's continued horror at my barmy decision-making process with a steady stream of light banter. Our progress through the rush-hour traffic was painfully slow but I was determined not to let my irritation show.

The school receptionist was waiting with Emily in the school car park as I pulled in through the gates at 6.15 p.m., her bright smile relieving some of the guilt I felt at keeping her after hours. After thanking her and apologising profusely, I climbed back into the car, the steady pulse of a foot in my back starting up the minute my seat belt was secured. Breathe, Rosie, breathe, I coached, focussing my attention on the glistening fields of rapeseed we passed as we drove towards home, and the tree-lined hills beyond.

Progress was still slow and we didn't pull into our quiet road until nearly quarter to seven. By then everyone was famished and, fearing that tempers were in danger of fraying, I decided not to ask Taylor about her mobile phone until she had eaten. I quickly fried some sausages and, after warming some beans and sprinkling them with grated cheese, I buttered some bread and asked Reece, who was circling, to help me carry everything through to the living room.

'What's this?' Taylor asked, staring down at the tray I held in front of her. She had changed out of her school uniform and was wearing a T-shirt with the word 'SEXY' emblazoned across the front. Skin-tight trousers and skirts barely six inches long seemed to be de rigueur for the girls at Taylor's school, and I could understand her wanting to fit in with the crowd, but blatant messages on clothes was a step too far, in my opinion. It wasn't the right moment to ask her to change though – there was enough tension in the air – so I bit my lip to stop myself from saying anything. Who on earth had bought a T-shirt like that for a child of her age, I wondered.

'Take it, quickly, honey,' I said. She could see exactly what it was.

'What? You serious? *This* is dinner?'

From somewhere deep inside I managed to locate and then project a breezy tone. 'Yep. If I'd had more time it would have been a bit more elaborate but as it is we're going to have to make do with a fry-up.'

Taylor looked at Emily, jaw hanging. She was trying to conjure up support. 'My God, she's reached a new low.'

Emily, through their joint love of craft and animals, seemed to have grown quietly fond of Taylor. As I sat down she threw Taylor a look of mild disapproval and then silently picked up her fork.

'I love beans, Rosie,' Reece said, trying to please. He was sitting on the floor in front of me and, taking my fork into my right hand, I patted his head affectionately with my left. He and Jamie then drifted into a giggly discussion about the effect of certain foods on the digestive system. Normally I would have steered them onto a more palatable conversation but it was such a relief to have something light to focus on that I left them to it. I still chewed mechanically though, convinced that Taylor hadn't quite finished her performance.

Sure enough, about five minutes later, when her plate was almost clear, she embarked on the finale. 'Well, that was the culinary equivalent of a car crash,' she said, swiping her wrist across her mouth and leaving a trail of tomato ketchup up her arm. 'In other words, crap.'

'Right, that's it! I've had enough!' I slammed my plate on the floor and leapt from the sofa, the placid part of my mind marvelling that she even knew the word culinary. 'Taylor, go up to your room. And I don't want to hear another word from any of you until you've finished your dinner!' At that moment, yelling felt good; a satisfying, blissful release.

Emily and Jamie, unused to hearing me shout, stared at me with their eyes boggling. Taylor made a big deal of leaving the room, a smug grin on her face. There was an air of triumph in her strut, as if she'd finally floored her opponent. Shaken by my sudden loss of temper, my heart thumped in my chest. I felt guilty about losing control in front of Emily and Jamie, something I rarely did, but it was Reece's reaction that really got to me, his stricken expression cutting me to the quick. With his hands clamped tightly over his ears, the top half of his body was folded over his knees as if braced for impact on board a turbulent flight.

I stood still for a moment, gathering myself. When Taylor finally disappeared from sight and my pulse had returned to its usual rhythm I dropped to my knees and patted between Reece's shoulder blades. 'I'm sorry for shouting, guys,' I said, turning to look at Emily and Jamie. 'It's been a long day but everything's going to be fine, OK?'

Reece straightened, his eyes filled with tears. 'She don't mean to be so horrible, Rosie.'

'Aw, I know, love, I know.' I kissed the top of his head. He really was a sweet child.

If it were possible to overdose on Bach's rescue remedy, I certainly did that evening. After dousing my tongue so liberally that all I could taste was metal, I held the small dark bottle under my nose and took several deep inhalations. Washing up the dishes helped to calm me enough to check on Taylor, puzzled as I was by the lack of noise coming from her room. I had come to associate her with commotion; she never closed a door if she could slam it and the floor vibrated whenever she drew near. Its absence made me nervous. For some reason I tiptoed up the stairs, unconsciously matching my own movements to the silence coming from her room. I pulled up short at the threshold to the bathroom, a flicker of movement drawing my attention. Taylor and I gasped simultaneously, our eyes fixed on the other's face. It was difficult to tell which of us was more shocked.

'W-what are you looking for?' I asked eventually, when I had found my voice. Taylor, who had been balancing on the rim of the bath and rummaging through the contents of the medicine cabinet, dropped the small box of plasters she had been holding. She jumped to the floor and straightened her top, her face brightly ablaze.

'Pills,' she said, eyeing me defensively. 'I got an 'eadache.'

'I don't keep painkillers in there,' I said in a strained voice, still recovering from the shock of what I'd glimpsed beneath her clothing when her top had lifted away from her jeans. 'Just plasters and bits and bobs. I'll get you something in a moment, but pop a jumper on over that T-shirt first, or put a different one on please. That one's not very nice, especially with younger children around.'

'What's wrong with it?' she asked, but she turned and went straight to her room. When she came out she was wearing a blue sweatshirt with 'BABE' printed in black letters on the front. The improvement, I thought, was marginal.

Churning with emotion, I put my hand on her shoulder as she passed by. She froze and then shuddered, as if my fingers were coated with slithers of ice. Immediately I withdrew, but then a fierce resolve gripped my stomach. I jogged along the hall after her, planted both hands on her shoulders and twisted her around to face me. Taken aback, her jaw dropped open.

'Taylor,' I said steadily, looking her in the eye. 'I couldn't help but notice those bruises on your side. They look nasty, honey. Who did that to you?'

Throwing her arms out to the side and then around, she shrugged me off. 'No one. They're nuffink, OK?' She tried to sidestep me but I took a step to the right, my legs a hip-width apart.

'No, it's not OK,' I insisted, annoyed with myself for using an antagonistic tone. I just couldn't believe that anyone would hurt a child so severely and I was struggling to contain my outrage. I gave my head a little shake. Why did our every interaction take the form of an argument? I took a breath and then continued more gently. 'I can see that you've been badly hurt,' I said, the image of her bruised and battered torso, visible when her T-shirt that had ridden up, was still pulsing on my retinas. With bruising like that, I wouldn't have been surprised if one of her ribs was broken. 'And I'm upset that someone has done that to you.'

'Oh for God's sake, it's nuffink. Someone pushed me over at school, all right?'

Concern boosting my determination to break through her brazen exterior, I blocked her path again as she tried to edge her way past, this time by raising my arm and pressing my hand flat against the wall. 'Taylor,' I warned gently. 'Come on, I'm not daft, love.'

She closed her eyes, looked away. After releasing a heavy sigh she turned back and fixed her gaze on my right ear.

'Well, it was like this, see,' she said, playing with the ends of her hair. 'There's this boy called Dash. That's literally his real name and I ain't lying.'

I raised my eyebrows. 'OK, go on.'

'And we got someone called Jet in our year as well, weird ain't it?'

I folded my arms. 'Taylor, please …'

'OK, OK,' she responded, holding up her hands. 'So basically, Dash likes me right, but this other girl thinks he's going out with her and so when he goes and sits next to me at break, she loses it big time and gets her mates to attack me. I dunno why 'cos I don't even like him. He thinks he's so cool but he ain't, he's creepy.'

'Creepy? In what way?'

'I dunno, just creepy.'

'Creepy as in he makes you nervous? Scared?'

She shrugged, tossing her hair over her shoulder with a shake of her head. 'I dunno do I? God-t! He just *is*.'

Convinced that she was using the rant as a smokescreen to distract me and refusing to be sidetracked, I ignored her bad language and recapped. 'So, a girl was upset with you and got some others to attack you. Where did this happen?'

Taylor glanced at me cagily. 'On the field, behind the hall. Why d'you wanna know?'

'Did anyone see it happen?'

She gave an unconvincing shrug. Someone saw all right, but she wasn't going to tell me who it was. After a pause she answered. 'Nah, no one.'

'So what did your teacher say?'

73

'Nuffink.'

'Nothing?! Those are pretty severe bruises, Taylor. I find it hard to believe they had nothing to say about it.' Something in the angle of her shoulders, the diffidence in her tone, told me that she was wavering, perhaps close to opening up about what really happened. Was she protecting one of her parents? Or perhaps both of them? Her loyalty, however misplaced, was honourable and I felt a rush of warmth towards her.

'I didn't tell no one, right?' She spoke with more certainty now and I knew that the moment of opportunity had gone. I felt irritated with myself for failing to inspire her to trust me. She shrugged her shoulders. 'Basically it'd happen all the time if I went round making a deal 'bout it. You don't have a clue.'

'Well I think we should mention something about it when we go back after the holidays.' I had to accept the possibility that she was telling the truth. If someone at school really had attacked her so violently, it couldn't be ignored. But then again, if one of her parents was responsible, it followed that little Bailey had been left in a highly volatile situation. If that was the case, I needed to let someone know about it, and soon.

Taylor folded her arms tightly across her chest. 'No need. The deputy went and suspended them girls what did it so it's sorted.'

I paused, unsure how to respond. Sensing a softening in my stance, she sidestepped me, heading for the stairs. She continued to chatter on as I followed her down, offering irrelevant, derogatory anecdotes about her classmates. I found myself nodding dumbly, my mind rewinding to something she had said days earlier. Hadn't she mentioned that the school field was out of bounds, fenced off because the roof of the hall was to be replaced?

In the living room she continued to trill on about how pathetic the other kids were and I listened absently, a feeling of melancholy settling on my chest. What chance had she had of forming positive relationships when her frame of reference came primarily from warring parents? The poor girl had no idea what a functioning, healthy relationship should look like and so her every interaction was threaded with abuse and confrontation. It was difficult to comprehend the depth of chaos she must have lived through.

I dearly wanted to let her know that I was on her side, that I wouldn't let anyone hurt her again. Keen to avoid being drawn into another argument, I sat a couple of feet away from her on the sofa, rehearsing what I wanted to say in my mind. Before I had a chance to formulate the words she had changed the subject completely, telling me, at lightning speed, about a project she needed to complete before the end of the holidays. 'We been reading *Charlie and the Chocolate Factory* and Miss Cooper says we gotta design this board game, right? But it has to have something to do with the book. Mum was gonna help me but –' At that moment Reece and Jamie charged in from the garden and her words were left hanging in the air.

Remembering something Des, my usual supervising social worker, had told me a couple of years earlier, I assured Taylor that I would help her with her project and then walked off into the kitchen. Soon after we first met, Des told me about a case he had been involved in, using it as an example of what can go wrong when inexperienced people stray beyond the parameters of their role. According to Des, an eight-year-old girl had confided in her teacher that she was being sexually abused by her uncle. Rather than immediately alerting social services and the police, the well-meaning teacher asked the child to repeat what she had said, using a camcorder to record the disclosure. Oblivious not only to the fact that she was jeopardising any future prosecution but also to the unnecessary stress she was placing on the young girl, the teacher prompted and encouraged her, believing she was being helpful. To Des's horror, the Crown Prosecution Service ruled that the child's evidence had been compromised and the offender was never charged with his crimes.

As I dried the dishes and put them away in the cupboard, our recent exchange came back to me. The more I thought about it, the more I couldn't help but admire the way Taylor had handled the situation. Without a hint of her usual hostility, she had guided me away from a subject she hadn't wanted to discuss and onto something she knew I would want to help her with. It struck me, with an uncomfortable thrum in my stomach, that she would do anything to protect the person who had hurt her.

Chapter Eight

Tired after the confrontation with Taylor and the endless redrawing of battle lines, I went to bed soon after the children that night, falling asleep almost immediately. I woke early on Friday, the first day of the Easter holidays, and got up as the sun was beginning to rise outside my window. Keen to write an incident report and send it off to Maisie before the children got up, I made a quick coffee and then returned to my room. I had called the out-of-hours social worker the night before to alert them to Taylor's injuries, but their advice had been to record everything and report to the office at 9 a.m. Since the dining table was in pieces under my bed, I knelt on the floor to sort through my paperwork, my hot drink beside me.

It was as I was flicking through the placement agreement looking for Taylor's date of birth that I realised the significance of the day. Cupping a hand to my cheek, I groaned – it was Reece's birthday and I'd had no idea. I felt a sudden rush of sympathy for him. I'd been so caught up in trying to get organised before the children broke up from school that I hadn't even thought to ask them when their birthdays were. Quickly, I found Taylor's details and let out a sigh of relief – her birthday wasn't until December.

In double-quick time I wrote a summary of Taylor's injuries including her account of how she sustained them and then pinged a copy off to Maisie in an email. Already I could hear movement upstairs so I dashed into the kitchen and rifled through the cupboards. Thankfully I found an unopened packet of balloons in one of the drawers and some bunting sandwiched between the top of the washing machine and the worktop.

Emily was the first downstairs. When she saw the decorations strung across the hall and around the living room she rubbed her eyes with her palms and then blinked, once, twice. 'What's going on, Mum?'

'It's Reece's birthday,' I whispered, handing her some balloons and a pump.

It was another fifteen minutes before the others came downstairs and by that time, Emily and I had managed to transform the living room so that it looked as if we'd been planning the celebration for a while, at least that's what I hoped. Reece's little face lit up and he smiled, that bright, sweet smile that grabbed me by the heart.

'Happy birthday, darling,' I said, brushing a kiss on his forehead.

He threw his arms around me so fervently that I nearly lost my footing. 'Owf,' I said, my voice bubbling with laughter. 'You're pleased with that I see.'

'Sorry, Rosie, sorry, sorry. Did I hurt you?' His joyful expression had transformed into one of concern.

'No, I'm fine,' I said, trying to hold my breath as he clung onto me. The sweetly stale smell of urine drifted up from his overfull nappy. 'Now, you pop to the bathroom and take your things off. I'll join you in a minute and then we'll have birthday pancakes for breakfast. How about that?'

That big beaming smile appeared on his face again, Emily and Jamie cheering behind him.

'We'll go shopping to choose you a present later.'

'Yeah!' He punched the air and then bumped shoulders with Jamie, who looked equally delighted.

'You could get Scalextric,' Jamie called out as Reece charged upstairs, rather deviously, I might add, since he had been longing for a set himself for some months.

Taylor, who had been glancing around the hurriedly decorated room with a sour expression, suddenly piped up: 'How much do I get?'

I turned around, the remnants of a smile still on my face. 'Sorry, honey?'

'What do I get to spend? The same as him?' She jerked her head towards the space her brother had just vacated.

'Um. Well, it's Reece's birthday, so it's his turn to get some presents today, but we can look for some new clothes for you, if you'd like to have a think about what you might need.' The local authority provided foster carers with a weekly allowance for clothes, which was supposed to be spent on clothing, whether it was needed or not. When children had been in care for several years, they tended to have more clothes than they knew what to do with. Most social workers allowed the money to be saved or spent on something else, but a few insisted on sticking to the guidelines. In truth, Taylor didn't really need any new clothes – her wardrobe was crammed full of designer-labelled garments and more shoes than I had ever seen in one room – but a fair number of them were inappropriate for a girl of her age. I was only too happy to buy her some items that didn't advertise her as 'JUICY' or declare her a 'BABE' or 'BOY MAGNET'. Secretly, I had hidden the worst offending items at the bottom of the ironing basket – it was like a black hole in there and could be months before they saw the light of day.

After establishing exactly how much she could spend, her frown relaxed a little, but she seemed far from happy. 'I've seen a diary with voice recognition that unlocks when you tell it to. I'm gonna get one of them.'

'Do you have enough money for that?'

'No but I'm gonna get it 'cos it's Reece's birthday, I told you. Dad always gets both of us presents when it's one of our birthdays. I'm basically allowed anything I want.'

I laughed, genuinely amused. 'Ha, yes, nice try, Taylor.'

The deep furrows on her brow and deepening flush rising from her chest, up her neck to her chin, told me there was nothing playful in our exchange, certainly not from her point of view. 'What's funny?'

'Ah-h, right, you're serious. Does your dad really get you both presents?'

She nodded slowly, as if not quite sure whether I was playing her along.

'Well, that's not the way we do things I'm afraid, Taylor, but like I said, you can choose some clothes if you'd like to.'

The flush crept over her chin and then quickly up to her hairline, her fury crackling like an empty pan on the hob. It was disturbing, the way she panted, her wild eyes locking onto mine like lasers. I decided to leave her like that, going tonto, and went up to see how Reece was getting on. In the bathroom, I soaped up a flannel to help him freshen up, slightly embarrassed to find that my hands were shaking. Was I really that cowed by a ten-year-old? It seemed ridiculous to think of a child in care as spoiled, but in a way Taylor was, materially at least. Handing Reece a towel, I wondered how their parents could possibly afford designer clothes and expensive birthday presents, when they were both apparently unemployed.

We were in the library later that day when Maisie called. 'Hello, just a second,' I whispered, aware of a disapproving glance from the children's librarian. I moved towards the exit and stood at the double doors so that the children were still in sight, cupping my hand over my mobile in an attempt to reduce the noise. 'Sorry, Maisie. Did you get my email?'

'So, yes, thanks for that. I've organised a police medical for Taylor later this afternoon. Four o'clock was the earliest the paediatrician could manage. Contact has been cancelled for the time being, until we've established what's happened.'

'Oh, that's a shame. It's Reece's birthday today.' I knew it couldn't be helped. Evidence of any assault had to be gathered at the earliest opportunity.

'So, yeah, right. Mum's been upset about the prospect of not waking up with him on his birthday, but frankly, that's tough. Those kids come first.'

I listened in silence for a moment, surprised by the realisation that I was beginning to like Maisie. Sometimes so hell bent on advocating for the children that she lost sight of common sense, I had felt that she wasn't terribly supportive, but there was no doubt that, like the vast majority of social workers, she cared deeply about the job she was doing. Anyone that fought to put children first couldn't be too bad, in my book.

After ending the call I walked over to Taylor. She was sitting on the floor and resting her head against one of the book shelves, her eyes closed. The others were rummaging through the many shelves, keen to choose some books to take home. Taylor simply wasn't interested; she looked bored out of her mind. Pretty certain that she'd be horrified, I decided not to break the news about the medical and cancelled contact until we got home, lest she went into one of her head-spinning, eye-boggling tantrums right below the sign that read 'QUIET PLEASE!'

Several carrier bags were strewn around her, the purchases going some way in soothing her ruffled feathers. Like many looked-after children, Taylor seemed to draw comfort from shopping – a short-lived opiate of the dissatisfied masses. Our local high street had proved disappointing to her though, accustomed as she assured me she was to shopping in the high-end boutiques on the edge of the next, larger town. Consumed by surface glitter, she had gazed covetously at the make-up and accessories counters in the department stores, seemingly genuinely amused when I told her that ten-year-olds shouldn't be worrying so much about how they looked.

'You're a lovely girl already, Taylor,' I had told her. 'You're funny and creative and loyal. You don't need all this *stuff*.' I wasn't trying to be antagonistic, just trying to make her stop and think for a moment. Was I really so out of touch, I wondered. Emily wasn't the slightest bit interested in fashion and neither were most of her friends, but perhaps they were unusual.

'Haven't you chosen anything yet?' I asked, crouching beside her and keeping my voice down. She was sulking because I'd refused to allow her to choose a book from the true-crime aisles in the adult section of the library. Drawn to anything and everything negative, it was her obsession with murderers that I found particularly unsettling.

'Nah, they're all boring.' She sniffed and grabbed one of the bags nearest to her, hugging it to her chest like a soft toy. 'I don't mind taking that one though.' She flipped a hard-backed book over with her pointed heel and then leaned her head back as if the effort really was too much. I reached for the book and straightened, turning it over in my hand. *The Goddess Girl's Book of Beauty*, boldly promising to be 'simply the most beautilicious guide out there'.

I suppressed a sigh. At home, hours were whittled away in front of the mirror as Taylor tried to perfect her appearance, but she never seemed happy with the result. Either that or she would flick her way through teen magazines (she had a whole pile of them under her bed), the proliferation of superficial articles bolstering her obsession with image – *Flirt Your Way to Success!* the cover lines screamed in glittery pink and gold letters, and *Celebrity What's Hot, What's Not*. There really was no escape. If she was to have a chance of being happy when she was older, I felt she needed to learn to define herself by other qualities, ones that she wouldn't lose with the passing years.

But then I remembered that reluctant readers often found non-fiction books more absorbing than novels. If a guide to beauty sparked an interest in reading, did it really matter so much? Beneath Taylor's hostile manner I sensed a sharp intelligence, emotionally at least. She certainly knew how to manipulate and I felt certain that if she channelled her energy into something more positive than obsessing about her looks, she might feel a little happier in herself.

Reece, I was pleased to see, was more than happy to spend part of his birthday in the library. He and Jamie shot occasional glances at each other across the shelves, seemingly competing over who could build the biggest pile of books to take out. Most of the ones he had chosen looked far too old for him but I had heard him read and he was more than capable. If it helped to keep his mind occupied and stopped him from posing all of those impossible questions, I didn't really mind what he read either.

Chapter Nine

It was Saturday morning when I finally brought up the subject of Taylor's mobile phone. The boys were in the garden, making the most of the gentle slope by rolling their cars from one end of the flagstone path to the other. My neighbours, Ted and Bernie, had bought Reece a remote control car after discovering that he'd recently had a birthday. 'I don't suppose he gets much, bless him,' they had said. It was such a kind gesture that I didn't like to tell them that, materially at least, children in care tended to get more presents than anyone else I knew.

With Emily tucked up in bed, unwell with a heavy cold, I decided to seize the rare moment of quiet and put some new cyberspace rules in place. Taylor was sprawled out on the sofa when I walked into the living room, her eyes fixed on the ceiling. She had been subdued since her medical, where all her injuries had been charted and the paediatrician had quizzed her as to how she'd received them.

Fiercely loyal, she had stuck to her original story, although like Chinese whispers, the facts were amorphous, changing when she was later questioned by a specially trained police officer.

Her only reaction, as I sat on one of the armchairs nearby, was a tiny flicker of her eyebrows. She didn't turn her head, even when I said her name. Preoccupied during breakfast and unusually quiet since then, I was hoping that I might have caught her in a peaceable mood. 'Tay-lor?' I said again, my voice rising at the end of her name.

'Mmmwha?'

I had never quite appreciated, until I met Taylor, how difficult it was to have a conversation with someone who showed complete disinterest in what I had to say. I found myself yearning over my knees to get closer to her, hoping to establish some connection, however tenuous, before continuing. She closed her eyes to block me out. 'We need to chat about your phone, honey,' I told her, masking my discomfort with an even tone.

Her eyes shot open and she turned sharply to look at me. 'What phone?'

'The mobile you've been using to talk to your mum.'

'I don't have no mobile,' she said, turning back to stare at the ceiling.

'Taylor, let's not make this difficult,' I said, trying to keep my voice from rising. 'I know you have one and that's fine. Absolutely fine. But social workers recommend that children keep their phones downstairs, not in their rooms. Don't worry, you can still use it, but we need to arrange certain times when you can speak to your parents, OK?'

Instantly outraged, she let out a loud, rasping groan and slapped her hands on her thighs. Taken by surprise, I almost jumped, but knowing that what Taylor most wanted was a reaction, I did my best to mask it, tilting my head to one side and drawing slowly back instead.

'Oh for God's sake, you're such a power-crazed bloody old witch.'

I looked at her for a moment, and then noticed Reece hovering in the doorway. I hadn't heard him come in from the garden so I wasn't sure exactly how long he'd been there. The child seemed to possess some sort of radar, appearing within moments of any disagreement. 'Hi, Reece,' I said, reassuring him with a thin smile. Taylor sat straight up when she heard her brother's name, her eyes firing invisible shards of ice across the room.

'I'm just having a little chat with Taylor. Nothing to worry about.'

He nodded. 'I heard. And she's lying! She does have a phone, Rosie. She told me I weren't allowed to say nothing.' Bless him, he couldn't help but tell the truth and though his sister was quivering with rage, I felt a little jolt of joy at the admission. When siblings come into care they often unite through the adversity. Reece loved his sister but, confident that I would treat her fairly, he had spoken out against her. That told me that he was feeling secure in the placement, something that meant a lot to me.

'Oh God,' Taylor spat with such ferocity that the 'd' actually sounded like a 't'. Spittle frothed at her mouth. 'You're such a stinking liar, Reece,' she screeched, launching herself across the room. Reece ducked out of the way and scrambled for the stairs, his sister charging after him and grabbing at the air with outstretched hands.

'Taylor, leave your brother alone,' I said, crisply. 'Now, come back here and calm down. There's no reason to get so worked up about this.'

She stamped back into the room, swinging her head wildly as she tossed her hair over her shoulder. Moments later Reece appeared in the doorway holding a phone aloft, a triumphant if slightly wary look on his face. 'See, Rosie. I weren't lying. Here it is.'

Taylor was across the room before I could react. She snatched the phone with one hand and lashed out with the other, catching Reece across the ear. He cried out, hand cupped tightly over the side of his head. 'Ow, Rosie,' he howled, tears streaming down his face. 'She hurt me.'

I drew him into a protective hug, relieved that he had made no attempt at retaliation. What would I have done if they had flown at each other again, I wondered. Toddlers scraping was one thing, but with Taylor barely an inch shorter than me and Reece taller than most six-year-olds, I wasn't sure who would come off worse. 'Taylor,' I snapped, talking over the top of Reece's head. 'You must learn to keep your hands to yourself. We don't hit in this house.'

She flicked her hair back, snorting with derision, and yet once again it was accompanied by a brief spasm of what appeared to be regret. 'He should learn to keep his trap shut then,' she told me, pointing at Reece. 'You wait,' she hissed, shaking her finger menacingly. 'You just wait till later. I'm literally gonna slice the skin off your face.'

My stomach rolled at her use of language. That sort of talk was disturbing enough in itself, but hearing it from the mouth of a child, and knowing, therefore, that she had heard it herself, chilled me to the core. Reece howled again, burrowing his head further into my shoulder. I pulled back and wiped his tears away with the pad of my thumb. 'Come on now, Reece. Go upstairs and get yourself a tissue.'

And then Reece's instinct for self-preservation kicked in. 'Dad said she could have it, Rosie. It weren't her fault,' he added, backtracking.

I patted his shoulder. 'Stop panicking, honey. We all need to calm down. Now, you pop upstairs and I'll be there in a minute.'

With one last anxious glance over his shoulder, he disappeared from view. I turned to Taylor and then decided to sit down, adopting a neutral stance. 'Right, shall we start again? There's no need to –' but before I could finish my sentence she held the phone out, offering it to me. Surprised, I stood up and stretched my hand out, palm upwards. She lowered the handset so that it brushed against my skin, but just as I began to close my fingers around it she whisked it away, leaving my hand hovering redundantly in mid-air.

'Come on,' I said, forcing a grown-up, conciliatory tone. 'Hand it over please.'

There was a nasty sneer on her face as she brandished it close to my face, once again snatching it away before I had chance to respond.

'Taylor,' I said warningly. Her air of superiority fuelled the irritation taking a hold in my chest and I felt my self-control slipping.

'Take it then,' she said teasingly, her head at a jaunty angle. 'You ain't trying hard enough.'

The myriad visions soaring through my mind, most of them involving me tussling with her for it, seemed to soothe me. Reminding myself that I was the adult, I turned, crossed the room and took a small box from the bureau beside her. Removing the lid, I laid the box gently on the mantelpiece and tried to claw back some authority, some sense of control. 'If your phone isn't in that box by the time I come back you'll lose your screen time for the next seven days.' I walked away, willing her to see sense.

In the kitchen I began scraping left-over porridge from some bowls with the edge of a spoon. The sticky, half-dried mixture was caked on but I worked tentatively, mentally bracing myself for further conflict. When children arrive in the foster home the source of their pain is often a mystery; social workers gather as much information as they can before a child is taken into care but it can take weeks in a safe environment before their full story emerges and they begin to calm down. Until then, foster carers have to deal with a tidal wave of emotions as they work through the shadows of what has gone on before.

Torn

I thought of Liz, a fostering friend of mine. The ex-head teacher had accepted a new placement a year earlier – a young boy of eight who had been registered since birth as a child in need by the local authority. Liz was told that Chayse had been neglected but was functioning well and had no particular behavioural issues. A few days into his stay it became clear that Chayse dealt with his inner pain by lashing out, his attacks random and unpredictable. For reasons that were at first unclear, car journeys seemed to trigger the most violent episodes, with Chayse wrapping his hands tightly around Liz's throat while she was at the wheel. His difficult behaviour ricocheted around the whole family, Liz's own children regularly falling victim to violent outbursts. It took several months before Chayse confided that his step-father had punished him by throwing him from a moving vehicle.

I grabbed a sponge and began scrubbing the worktops, realising that, once again, my hands were trembling. There was a spitefulness to Taylor's behaviour that was disturbing and I was beginning to suspect that domestic violence wasn't the only issue in the Fielding household. There was a loud bang in the living room, followed by a moan and another crash. Weeks earlier the noises would have had me barrelling in to see what was wrong but I had learnt to ignore most of what went on; noisy chaos was the timpani of Taylor's day.

Intent as I was in blitzing the kitchen to distance myself from the exasperation stewing in the pit of my stomach, I couldn't say how much later it was that I heard heavy footsteps on the stairs. She always sounded as if she was wearing hobnail boots, the treads creaking and groaning under her feet. I do remember feeling hopeful, as I rinsed my hands under the tap, that when I walked into the living room the phone would be sitting in the box I had left out. To my joyous relief it was there – a black handset that looked so thin I wondered whether it was actually real. I picked it up, surprised at how light it felt in the flat of my hand. Motorola RAZR was emblazoned across the top, the letters so shiny that it appeared to be brand new. Not for the first time, I found myself wondering how unemployed parents could afford to lavish their children with such expensive gadgets and gifts.

After lunch, while I was in the kitchen loading some whites into the washing machine, Taylor offered to do the drying up. She had hardly spoken a word to anyone since our disagreement and so I stopped what I was doing and stared at her, wondering what she was up to.

It was clear in the way she looked at me and the shadows passing across her eyes that her heart wasn't really in it, but whatever her reasons, I was happy to go along with a truce. 'That would be great, thank you.'

We spent the next twenty minutes or so moving awkwardly around one another in the kitchen, her drying up and putting crockery away in cupboards, me folding clothes and sorting them into piles. 'Can I use the computer when I've finished doing this?' she asked. Oddly mechanical in her politeness, I got the sense that she was going through the motions because she had come to realise that life was easier that way.

'Of course, yes. You're not allowed on Myspace though. You have to be fourteen to go on there.' Karron was correct about that – I had checked.

An invisible film of ice crept over her eyes. She stared at me for a moment, nostrils flaring, but then she gave me a curt nod and turned away, perhaps deciding it was too soon to launch into another battle. For the rest of the afternoon she sat staring at the computer screen, her finger barely moving from the mouse as she continually refreshed the live Chelsea score. Towards the end of the second half she grew increasingly agitated, so much so that she could no longer sit down. When the final whistle blew and I asked her the score she actually smiled at me, her joy at Chelsea's win palpable.

'You're quite a fan aren't you?'

'Meh,' she said with a shrug. Staring at her feet, she said: 'Actually, Rosie, I'm sorry about earlier and the phone. I shouldn't of messed you around like that.'

However rehearsed the speech sounded, her high-pitched, strained tone revealed just what an effort it took to make it and when I said 'Thank you, Taylor, I'm grateful for that' I meant it.

'Can I call Mum?' she asked, and her voice unusually light and warm. Looking back, I think her ability to transform her mood so easily was one of the things about her that unsettled me most. She was a strong character, there was no doubt about that, but the essence of her was amorphous. In terms of getting to know her, I felt we were still in the foothills, merely treading water. I suspected that we had barely skimmed the surface of her true character.

'Well, Maisie said your telephone contacts should be on Mondays and Thursdays, so how about we swap one of those with today? Are you happy with that?'

Without looking up, she moved one of her shoulders in a meek shrug.

When the call connected Taylor pottered from the living room to the hallway and then the kitchen, keen to avoid being overheard. I planted myself on the sofa and feigned interest in a TV magazine, my eyes fixed unseeingly on one page as I strained to hear the conversation. Before handing the phone to Taylor I had activated the loudspeaker function, but, tech-savvy, she must have quickly adjusted the volume because I could barely make out Claire Fielding's voice.

Her mother's tone was unmistakably timid though, I could tell that much. Every time she spoke Taylor cut her off, speaking with even more asperity than usual. 'Well, when then?' she demanded, striding from room to room and gesticulating with her free hand. There was a low muttering and then Taylor jumped in. 'But you promised that last month, and the month before that.'

I tilted my head towards her, clueless as to what she was talking about. Considering how adoring she sounded whenever she spoke of her mum, I was taken aback by her caustic tone.

Torn

'But you're always saying that and it never happens. You're so bloody useless!' Shocked, I couldn't help but look up. Taylor was oblivious. She threw her free arm up in the air and turned in a tight circle, continuing with the tirade. 'Why can't you do anything right?' she growled. 'There's always some excuse. Can't do it this week – Reece isn't feeling well. Can't do it next week – Bailey has to see the doctor.' In full swing, Taylor rocked her head from side to side and pecked at the air with her hand. 'Blah, blah, blah-de-blah. It makes me sick, Mum.'

There was a low-pitched squeak followed by staccato breathing at the other end of the line. It sounded to me as if her mother was crying. All of a sudden the tempo changed. Taylor, her whole demeanour softening, began to make soothing noises, running her free hand anxiously through her hair. Whispering words of comfort, her own voice became tremulous, unrecognisable to me. The call ended soon afterwards and when I got up and went into the kitchen, Taylor was standing quietly with her eyes closed, her head pressed against the fridge.

Chapter Ten

It was almost lunchtime on Monday, two days after Taylor's meltdown over the phone restrictions, and the morning was going pretty much as expected. Sitting in the local authority offices, I listened as our tutor, a tired-looking man named Ken, with trousers that were too short and damp patches on his shirt, explained that the time-out technique made famous by 'Supernanny' Jo Frost should only be used as a last resort in managing difficult behaviour. 'Ostracising a child who already feels like an outsider is counterproductive,' he told us in monotone. 'It does nothing to build their self-esteem, which is ultimately what all of us should be trying to achieve.'

'It works though,' said the dark-skinned woman sitting next to me. Like me, she had grown increasingly fidgety throughout the morning. Every so often she withdrew a pack of Rolos from her bag, throwing me a subversive smile as she offered one to me. She ate them two at a time, presumably to alleviate the monotony.

Torn

'It may well do at first,' Ken told her, sounding slightly affronted at the suggestion. 'But the more you use it the less effective it will be. And how do you make a child of six take time-out if they don't want to?' He glanced around the small group of foster carers arranged on a semi-circle of chairs in front of him and then answered his own question before any of us could reply. 'I'll tell you how. By man-handling them. And I'm sure I don't need to tell you how much trouble that can get you into.'

'What are we supposed to do when they're naughty then?' a well-dressed woman sitting at the end of the row asked, a badge with the name Valerie stuck to her top. I couldn't tell how old she was, but I guessed she was edging towards the end of middle age, not much younger than my own mother. Of an era when children were expected to behave without incentives, I wondered whether she considered modern soft discipline to be, in the words of my mother, 'a lot of silly nonsense'. Mum was of the opinion that cajoling children into behaving was akin to negotiating with terrorists and should never be done. Anyone who believed in reasoning with young children, to her mind, wasn't to be trusted.

My tummy rumbled in protest as Ken reached for a chair, dragged it closer to his audience and made himself comfortable. Lunch had just slipped further away. Valerie, apparently alarmed to be singled out for special attention, leaned so far back in her chair that its front legs left the floor. A hotbed of irrelevant questions, instant coffee and stale air, local authority training courses were rarely a source of comedy and so, glassy-eyed and restless, when the man sitting opposite me rolled his eyes and stifled an exaggerated yawn I was overcome with an almost irrepressible need to giggle.

'And so "naughty" really is such an unhelpful word,' Ken stated at the end of a ten-minute monologue. Apparently, 'don't' and 'no' were words to be avoided as well. 'You should always try and frame a request in the positive, so instead of saying "Don't touch that" change the emphasis, perhaps telling the child what they are allowed to handle. And if you really must label behaviour, it's better to refer to it as non-compliant. Far more descriptive and less condemning, do you see?' He leaned forward in his chair, directing the question at Valerie. She tilted her head slightly in polite acknowledgement but her compressed lips and stiffened shoulders suggested that she didn't *see* at all.

Ken announced our lunch break with a brisk slap to his thigh, clearly satisfied that he had provided a distinguished argument. The saving grace of the whole course came mid-afternoon, when our lecturer moved on to tell us about children who were forced to swap roles with their parents, taking on family responsibilities inappropriate to their age. Ken told us that there were all sorts of reasons why parents shifted responsibility to younger members of the family – substance misuse, mental or physical illness, neglect – and because they were left to care for younger siblings as well as parenting the adults, children in those situations were often perceived as controlling and bossy. After running a household single-handedly, young carers sometimes struggled to adjust to life in the foster home, where their childhood was offered back to them. Ken went on to say that children who have parented their parents remained so fiercely loyal that even acknowledging their foster carer feels like betrayal.

Remembering Taylor's telephone call with her mother, the hair on my forearms prickled. Towards the end of the conversation mother and daughter had reversed roles; Claire tearfully sulky and Taylor trying to soothe her with a placating tone. Putting on a brave front in front of her children didn't seem to be something Claire Fielding did and when Ken went on to say that young carers were often mature beyond their years and seemingly resilient, it was as if he was talking about the ten-year-old personally.

Around 4 p.m. Ken told us that foster carers looking after children who use violence should respond mildly, using the mantra 'kind hands', until the message seeps into their psyche. Next to me, Valerie heaved a weary sigh and my mind, having reached saturation point, began to drift. I wondered how my mum was coping with Taylor. My official back-up carer, my mother had volunteered to look after the children so that I could attend the course, and I knew that she wouldn't tolerate any of what she would describe as 'cheek'.

If the journey over to her house that morning was anything to go by, she wasn't in for an easy time of it. It had been fraught, Taylor and Reece bickering and elbowing each other in the back of the car, as they had the previous day, when we'd taken a spur of the moment trip to the coast. As Taylor and Reece rolled up their trousers to paddle, it was a relief to see they weren't black and blue from the journey. Boredom and confined spaces were never a good mix when it came to children, but for these siblings, it was a particularly explosive cocktail.

A believer in good old-fashioned authoritarianism and never one to hold back, Mum regarded me as outrageously soft so I was slightly nervous about how she would deal with them should something trigger one of Taylor's meltdowns.

So when I arrived at her house to pick them up at 5.30 p.m I was more than a little surprised to find the pair of them kneeling side by side in the garden, planting Gladioli bulbs. Emily, Jamie and Reece were lounging around in the living room, watching television. As soon as he set eyes on me Reece raced over and put his arms around my middle, his face awash with emotion. 'Rosie!' he screeched, wiggling his front tooth between finger and thumb. 'Rosie, my tooth is all wobbly!'

I kissed the top of his head. 'Oh, you're going to look too cute when you're toothless,' I said with a grin.

'How exactly did you manage that?' I asked Mum later as we stood in her small galley kitchen. The comforting smell of apple and cinnamon rose from the oven and I closed my eyes for a second, savouring it. The children were in the dining room tucking into chicken casserole with roast potatoes, a meal mum had prepared to save me having to cook when I got home.

'What?' she asked, raising her shoulders in a shrug, but her eyes were twinkling. She knew I'd been struggling with Taylor and it was sort of a running joke between us – her ability to build an instant rapport with the children in my care, while I was often left floundering behind. The old adage that it took a village to raise a child couldn't be truer, when it came to fostering. It wasn't just me looking after the children; my family and friends all played an invaluable part. 'She's been as good as gold all day. I honestly couldn't fault her.'

I let out a breath, shaking my head and smiling ruefully.

'Oh don't look like that,' she said consolingly, the laughter still lingering in her eyes as she pushed her glasses further up on the bridge of her nose. 'It's easier for them to accept me; I'm not taking the place of their mum so there's none of that conflict. No divided loyalties.' By 'them', Mum was referring to my first placement, a sibling group of three, each a year apart and all under the age of five. Early on in the placement the eldest two, a girl and boy, seemed convinced that I'd kidnapped them, howling whenever I went anywhere near. 'Look at Freya and Flynn; they thought the world of you, in the end.'

I pressed my lips together. 'Hmm, it's the beginning and middle bit I seem to struggle with.'

Mum tittered and patted my arm. 'Oh, before I forget,' she said, tightening her grip. 'Taylor tells me she hasn't got any pyjamas and she gets cold at night. Is that true? Because if you need to borrow a few bob to get her some you know I've got that money I'm saving for Christmas –'

I buried my face in my hands, shaking my head. 'Oh Mum, I don't believe that girl!' Since separating from Gary, Mum seemed to think I was destitute and was always offering to help me out, even though she had little herself. 'We went out a day or two ago and I bought her two new pairs of pyjamas. Her drawers are brimming with them anyway! What on earth does she get out of saying things like that?'

'Ooh, what a little cow! I've a mind to have a word with her.'

I grabbed her arm. 'No, Mum, I think it's best left alone.'

She nodded and then her eyebrows shot up. 'Ah, there was something else as well, something odd.'

'Ri-ght?' I said slowly.

'It was something Reece said earlier. He was messing around with Taylor and he called her, "sexy".' Mum wiggled her arthritic index fingers up and down when she said the word, wincing a little. 'Bold as brass he was. I told him not to say things like that and he said, "Why not? Daddy says she is."'

I stilled. 'Did he mean his dad says it to Taylor?'

'Well, now you're asking me.' She cupped her chin and frowned, her eyes moving slowly from side to side. 'I couldn't rightly say. I was a bit shocked, tell you the truth. Why would a father say that, of all things? And to his own daughter?'

Why indeed? I thought. But then I checked myself. One of the girls in Emily's class was called Lexi and she was widely referred to, even by some of the parents, as 'Sexy Lexi'. While it seemed wildly inappropriate to me, it was a current fashion to refer to everything as sexy, even houses and cars. It was wise for foster carers to nurse a heavy dose of doubt but it could lead to tunnel vision. Determined to keep an open mind, I gave my head a little shake and looked back at my mum. For the first time I noticed how tired she was looking. 'Are you feeling OK? You look a bit pale.'

Soon after I began fostering a couple of years earlier, Mum found a lump in her breast. Selfless to a fault, she only told myself and my brothers that it was malignant two nights before she was due to have an operation, and only then because she needed me to look after her cat. I was sure that if she could have dealt with the whole business discreetly, including the extensive treatment that followed, she would have spared her children the worry.

Predictably, she grabbed the tea-towel draped over her shoulder and fluttered it through the air. 'Oh, don't start fussing about me, Rosie,' she answered, dismissing my concern with a note of finality. 'I'm absolutely fine.'

Even when chemotherapy had taken its toll, laying her low, she had shielded the three of us from the worst of it. Once again I thought about Taylor's telephone conversation with her mum. How unfair it was that someone so young had been exposed to the harsh realities of life rather than insulated by her parents, when others were given so much, with little expected in return.

Chapter Eleven

The next morning I surprised the four of them by announcing that we were going on a day trip. Sitting side by side in the living room, they were halfway through eating their breakfast when I told them I had booked tickets for a tour of Cadbury World, a chocolate museum in Birmingham. 'As soon as you've finished eating we'll set off. I've packed a picnic, so we're all set to go.'

'Oh God, no-wer. I'm too tired to go out-er,' groaned Taylor, half-reclined on the sofa.

'I thought you'd be *pleased*,' I said, trying to disguise my disappointment with fake cheer. 'You have to get your *Charlie and the Chocolate Factory* project done by the end of the holidays. You never know, this might spark a few ideas.'

Taylor dropped her head forward, her long fringe covering her face. It was something she did whenever she was displeased and I had grown used to talking to a curtain of hair. After a moment she ran her fingers through the thick roots, first with the left and then the right, finally dragging them back through her scalp so that I could hear the stomach-churning sound of nails scraping through skin, hair pulled taut as it went. 'What you looking at me like that for?' she snapped. I decided not to answer. 'Today is officially the worst day of my life.'

'But I thought yesterday was the absolute worst day ever?' I said, trying to sound light and breezy.

'Yeah, well, that's 'cos there's so many to choose from around here,' she said gravely. 'I'm literally spoilt for choice.'

Though I was loath to admit it, Taylor was quite witty, and in other circumstances I might have giggled.

'You look nice, Rosie,' Reece said, over an hour later when I came downstairs after getting dressed – Taylor had spent so long getting ready that the rest of us had to make do with a quick wash. Using the bathroom after her was a risky business, the air so saturated with deodorant that I was almost asphyxiated by lingering fumes. When she finally came downstairs she resembled Betty Boop; her lashes so spider-like and sticky with mascara that they clung together whenever she tried to blink.

In response to her brother's compliment she gave a derisory snort, her eyes sweeping over me with a look of distaste. I was wearing jeans, a T-shirt and an old cardigan but I knew it didn't really matter what I had on; Reece, as usual, was desperately trying to make up for Taylor's earlier negativity. 'You are sweet, Reece,' I said, laughing and giving him a hug. 'Visually challenged but sweet.'

Reece looked bemused as I kissed the top of his head.

'If that means half-blind then I agree,' Taylor muttered, pulling her lips in and massaging them with a loud sucking sound. Her hair was now drawn tightly back so that the V of her widow's peak was more pronounced than ever, her painted cheeks glowing scarlet. She smirked, examining her fingernails.

'What can I say, Taylor? It's touching that you give me so much thought.'

Her head shot up but I walked into the kitchen to fill some empty bottles with water for the journey before she could say anything else. Her comments were jarring, like foil on a filling, but I was glad that she directed her venom my way instead of towards the other children. Though Jamie tended to avoid her, she and Emily got on brilliantly; an attraction of opposites I think. If Taylor spoke to them the way she did to me, I'm not sure I could have handled it so calmly.

Fearing that Taylor might conduct a sit-in at home (the thought obviously hadn't occurred to her), I was relieved to finally get them all in the car. Glued to the computer screen, she had waited until the last possible moment before resentfully shoving her feet into her shoes, and I was beginning to suspect that part of the reason for her reluctance to leave the house was her attachment to cyberspace.

Dropping my usual guard against thoughtless comments, after securing my seat belt I turned around and said: 'Now, let's have a nice peaceful journey. No squabbling like last time.' I closed my eyes, realising my mistake before my words took effect – all I had done was remind them of their last in-car row, more or less telling them to resume where they left off. It was then that I realised the value of our lecturer's advice, when he told us to avoid negative words such as 'no' and 'don't'.

Within seconds an argument was in full swing, Taylor and Reece both fighting over how much space the other was taking up. 'Look, here's the line!' Taylor shrieked, slicing her hand through the air like a guillotine. 'You keep your arms in your own air space and stop elbowing me!'

Reece began to cry. 'That's not fair, Rosie,' he sobbed, 'she's got more room than me.'

'Oh, for goodness sake!' I said, irritated with myself as much as them. I took a soothing breath and then chirped: 'Tell you what. Let's play a game!' Even one of Reece's torturous car games was preferable to a screaming match. 'How about "I Spy"?'

'I wanna read my book,' Reece said, hiccoughing back a sob and wiping his eyes with the palm of one hand. Throwing Taylor one last wounded look, he buried his head in his book. 'I spy with my little eye, something beginning with C ...,' said Jamie. Emily and I began to make suggestions but Taylor refused, staring moodily out of the window. Moments later Reece began bobbing up and down in his seat, hand raised as if in the classroom. 'What is it, Reece?' I asked, after Emily correctly guessed 'clouds'.

'Do you know why some people call their toilet a "cloakroom", Rosie?'

A vague glimmer of knowledge began to surface in my mind but I shook my head, not wanting to spoil his fun.

'Because in the olden days people used to hang their cloaks over the toilet so that the stink would kill the fleas.'

'Yuk!' I exclaimed and he laughed out loud.

'Cool!' said Jamie.

Reece looked delighted. 'And did you know that people used to poop in the street? The roads were full of turds and –' He stopped, his head jerking sideways. 'Hey, Taylor. That's the dentist you went to when you cracked your tooth ain't it?'

'Mm-mmn-mn,' Taylor mumbled in the tone of 'I don't know', but she followed it with a warning grunt and, I noticed when I glanced in the rear-view mirror, a deadly stare. Her eyes shot to mine and then she looked quickly away.

'Yes you do!' he insisted, forehead puckered. 'When Mummy cooked the money by accident and you bit into it.'

'Oh for God's sake, shut it, Reece.' Taylor sounded angry but her expression told a different story – it was agonised, fearful even. I felt a brief tug at my heart.

'Cooked some money?' I repeated, trying to keep my voice light. Recalling something a prison officer friend of mine had told me, I became aware of a creeping sensation along my forearms. 'Do you mean money in a Christmas pudding?'

'Na!' Reece said, laughing. 'It was sketty Bolognase. Mummy dropped some pound coins in the pan by accident when she was cooking and Taylor got it in her dinner.

We're not allowed to tell Daddy that though. Shhh, Rosie.'
Exaggeratedly, he put his fingers to his lips and gave his
sister a defiant stare. 'It's all right, Taylor. Daddy can't hear
us.'

Cadbury World was located in a large manor house on the
outskirts of Bournville, a quintessential English village.
The imposing, red-brick mansion with uneven timber
beams and narrow dormer windows sat just beyond a wide
green, flanked on either side by several tall fir trees, its
backdrop tumbledown fields of brown and green. The
surrounding gardens were striking and Taylor, who rarely
had a good word to say about anything, oohed and aahed
her way past the hollyhocks, rhododendrons and hydran-
geas. With the happy, carefree smile of childhood reaching
her habitually sad eyes, I felt my discomfort slowly melting
away.

Inside, the doors were heavy and ornamental, the rooms
panelled with the dark oak reminiscent of old-fashioned
courtrooms. As I rummaged around in my handbag for the
tickets that I had printed at home, Reece's excitement was
heading towards fever pitch. Clutching my forearm, he
bobbed manically around on his toes. Knowing that an
avalanche of questions was heading my way, I was pleased
to discover that we were able to make our own way around
in a self-guided tour. At least we wouldn't disturb anyone
else.

Each room was large, the walls decorated with vintage
posters and boards telling the story of the Quaker family

and Cadbury's chocolate. During the first part of the tour we were offered samples of 80 per cent cocoa solids chocolate so bitter that we all shuddered and equally jarring watery liquid chocolate, served cool in a tiny glass. There were lots of interactive displays and activities to keep the boys occupied, all manned by enthusiastic staff who didn't seem to mind Reece bombarding them with questions.

After a couple of hours he seemed to have burnt himself out, he and Jamie walking quietly beside me while Taylor and Emily lagged behind. I could tell that they were all enjoying themselves because their regular habits temporarily vanished; Jamie went a whole two hours without using Americanisms, slipping only when he referred to a set of particularly heavy looking curtains as drapes. Reece managed a whole conversation without screwing his eyes up and twitching, and Taylor smiled whenever I pointed anything out to her, even responding occasionally in a pleasant tone.

Lovely as it was to see them so absorbed, I couldn't quite relax. My thoughts kept returning to our car journey and Reece's comment about the coins. I longed to talk to Taylor about it, but I knew that, even if I engineered the opportunity, it was unlikely that she'd want to confide in me. Every time I glanced at her my stomach pulsed with a regular, discomforting thrum. Help me understand, I wanted to say.

'That was *so* cool,' she said as we made our way to the car, her chin bearing the remnants of the free samples she had taken full advantage of. 'I wanna go back in and start all over again.'

Torn

Inured as I was to sarcasm, I almost started at the pleasant tone in her voice.

When we got home it was still warm outside so Emily, Jamie and Reece went straight into the garden. Taylor hung around me, being nice, and then asked if she could use the computer. 'Of course,' I said, 'but just to check your emails. It's lovely outside. We may as well make the most of it.' Her chest seemed to sag a little at that, relieved at getting her online fix.

Twenty minutes or so later, after some gentle coaxing from me, she left the screen and joined the others in the garden. The boys were playing Swingball, though a distinct lack of co-ordination meant they were ducking the ball more often than hitting it. Emily was stretched out on the grass a safe distance away, one hand behind her head, the other clutching a book. Taylor lolled beside her, examining her nails from every angle. Periodically she held her hands together at full stretch, tilting her head as if comparing one set of fingers with the other.

Time was getting on so I cooked a simple tea; hot dogs in rolls with salad and noodles. After setting some water in a saucepan to boil, I stood at the back door, butterflies whirling close by. This is the life I dreamed of having, I thought, as I watched the girls jump to their feet and cartwheel across the grass. The boys, abandoning their game, charged over and joined in, the four of them tumbling over one another and laughing helplessly. The evening was still with just the tiniest breeze and suddenly I felt warm inside, filled with optimism.

An unfamiliar tinkling sound rising above their peals of laughter caught my attention – in the living room, Taylor's mobile telephone was ringing from its position in the box on the mantelpiece. The phone vibrated in my hand when I picked it up, something I hadn't expected at all. All four children were still crouched over, wheezing with uncontrollable laughter when I called out to them. 'Taylor,' I shouted, having spoken briefly to Claire, 'your mum's on the phone, honey.'

Instantly, Taylor's smile vanished and she fell into a hunch like an old lady. Shuffling over, she took the handset without looking at me and breathed a weary 'hello'. Her voice loaded with gravitas, she told her mum that she had done 'nuffink' all day and was thoroughly bored. Reminded immediately of Andy, the character in *Little Britain* who, unbeknown to his carer, Lou, feigns the need for a wheelchair, I could almost have laughed, had it not been quite so irritating.

When I caught sight of her sheepish expression as she handed the phone back to me, though, my heart softened. Torn between their innate need to belong and a fierce sense of loyalty towards their parents, it was rarely easy for children to relax in care. Acutely aware of her mother's feelings, I saw the struggle pass over Taylor's eyes every time they spoke and, as much as it was annoying, it was also tragic that so many complications were impinging on her childhood. As so often happens in fostering, I was struck by how helpless I was – there wasn't an awful lot I could do to lighten her load.

We sat on the grass, eating our food picnic-style and later on, when the garden was in shadow and I'd cleared everything away, we all sat down to watch one of Taylor's favourite programmes – a fly-on-the-wall documentary about sick animals and the vets caring for them. On the screen, a Labrador puppy was laying stretched out in his tearful owner's arms, his right ear half-severed and bloody after an attack by a German Shepherd. Taylor's hands flew to her cheeks and stayed there, her eyes misty with tears. My eyes kept drifting from the screen to steal surreptitious glances at her, reassured to see proof that there was a soft side in there somewhere; that, essentially, she was a sweet, kind person.

'Our dog looks a bit like that,' she said, when the puppy had been treated and she was relieved enough to tear her eyes from the screen. She sounded young when she said it, her voice soft and free from its usual brittleness. 'He's a cross between a Staffie and a Boxer.'

'Ooh, sounds like a scary combination,' I said, being wary of large dogs myself.

'No! Not at all, he's soppy. Mum says he's frightened of his own shadow.'

I laughed.

Reece, sitting at my feet with his head resting against my knees, turned around to look at me. 'Yeah, he hates it when Mum –'

'Shut it, Reece,' Taylor snapped, hurriedly glossing over the moment as if I wouldn't be able to guess what her brother was about to say. Words spilling over themselves, she then told me about the day they went to a rescue centre. 'Mum couldn't resist him,' she said, her voice brimming with affection. 'He looked so sad.' Her lower lip jutted out and, gripped by a sudden warmth, I patted her leg unthinkingly. When I realised what I'd done I steeled myself for some sort of reaction but I was surprised to find that there wasn't one. No recoiling or disgusted grunt. And then she surprised me again, turning towards me and saying: 'I s'pose fostering's a bit like taking in rescue dogs isn't it?' She sounded so unlike the brusque, over-confident child I was used to that it was like sitting with a different person entirely.

'Hmm, not quite!' I exclaimed.

Her forehead puckered. 'What made you want to look after other people's kids?'

'Ooh, ask a question like that and you're going to get a cheesy answer. Are you ready for it?' She rolled her eyes and nodded. Emily and Jamie grinned. 'I like helping people; it's as simple as that really. Especially children.'

'What? Even kids like me?' She chewed the side of her lip and looked away as she waited for an answer, unusually hesitant.

'*Especially* kids like you,' I replied, which was true in lots of ways. Apart from relishing the challenge, the frustrated nurse in me longed to root out Taylor's wounds and soothe them away. She gave me a shy, genuine smile, the sort that made me realise why I loved being a foster carer.

Over the next half an hour we whizzed through the best bits of *The Wizard of Oz*, all four children joining in as

Dorothy chanted, 'There's no place like home, there's no place like home.' Taylor and Reece were both smiling but I felt a catch in my chest, wondering if they ached with homesickness as I had, whenever I'd visited an unfamiliar place as a child.

After the boys had gone to bed, I tried to find a film that would appeal to both Taylor and Emily. 'How about *Hellbreeder*, Rosie? Have you seen that?' Taylor asked. Not for the first time I got the impression that it had been open season at home, both online and on the television, with the children being allowed to watch whatever they wanted, whenever they liked. And what Taylor wanted was horror, the gorier the better.

'Oh goodness, no. *Pirates of the Caribbean* was enough to give me nightmares. Was *Hellbreeder* any good?'

'Nope. Worse film ever.'

After much discussion we watched *The Parent Trap*, the film an immediate hit with Taylor. At the end, when the fractured family was reunited, Taylor's eyes were once again damp, this time with happy tears. 'What a load of crap,' she pronounced as the credits rolled, but asked if she could take charge of the remote control nevertheless, rewinding the last scene and watching it over and over again. 'That stinks,' she declared, after the seventh viewing. 'There's no such thing as a happy ending.'

'That's not true. I can think of lots of happy endings,' I said, trying to redress the balance in her mind. She was such a prophet of doom. 'I know lots of happy people with happy lives.'

'Like who?'

I patted my chest. 'Like me, for a start. I'm happy.'

'Me too,' Emily piped up. At least, that's what it sounded like – she was still very bunged up from her cold.

'Yeah, well, you might be at the moment, but neither of you are dead yet, so it don't count as the end.'

I laughed, tilting my head one way then the other. 'Hmm, can't argue with that I suppose.'

'But you never know. Literally any day could be your last,' she added.

My smile melted away. 'You really are a little ray of sunshine, aren't you, Taylor?'

'Just saying,' she said, with a twisted smile. 'It probably won't end well.'

It was an idyllic evening, one of those to reminisce about in those painful, disorienting days after a placement ends. I think we all went off to our rooms feeling content that night, which is why I was so shocked to find, late on Sunday evening, an email in my inbox entitled 'COMPLAINTS', marked by Maisie as urgent.

Chapter Twelve

Sleep evaded me that night, the list of complaints made by Claire, the sibling's mother, scrolling up and down in front of my eyes like a sadistic autocue. From continually plying the children with nothing but junk food to refusing them painkillers when they were unwell, there were seven accusations in total, each criticising a different aspect of what social services term as 'standards of care'. One of them was easy to dismiss – Claire's claim that I had neglected to buy the children the clothes they needed. Without checking back through my records I couldn't say exactly how much I had spent on them but I knew it was far more than the allowance given to me by the local authority. Thankfully, having kept all of the receipts from our shopping trips, I had evidence to prove it.

But how could I defend myself against the others? One accusation was that I shouted at the children, making them feel intimidated. In truth, I had raised my voice in frustration several times, but Taylor had barely blinked. She certainly hadn't been cowed enough to do as I had asked. Adding insult to injury, she also claimed that I frequently turned up late to collect her from school – of all the complaints, I was livid over the irony of that one, still fuming as I stood in front of my wardrobe, trying to decide what to wear.

The children's first LAC review had been organised for 10 a.m. that morning at the local authority offices. When meeting parents, I always tried to make a good impression, but in the light of the complaints it seemed even more important. In the end I chose a fitted blouse and a tailored skirt, the outfit I had worn two years earlier to meet the fostering panel.

I had replied to Maisie's email late the previous evening, giving a detailed response to each complaint and bringing her up to date with what the children had said over the last couple of days, to myself and my mother. I couldn't go into detail about Taylor's cracked tooth, but I was hoping to get a chance to talk to Maisie alone after the meeting.

Just after 8 a.m., while the children were having breakfast (porridge with fruit and honey, much to Taylor's disgust), I was surprised to find that the social worker had already replied, thanking me for my prompt response and reassuring me that she herself saw no grounds for concern.

Reece was even more skittish than usual as we drove towards my mother's house to drop Emily and Jamie off. Concentrating hard on getting myself in the right mindset, I was quieter as well, trying to swallow down the righteous defensiveness at being accused of providing poor care. When we arrived at Fargate House Reece climbed out of the car and, his cheeks pulsing in violent twitches, tugged at my sleeve. 'I don't want to,' he whispered, close to tears.

'What? Go to the meeting, you mean?'

He nodded, tears spilling onto his cheeks.

I cupped his cheeks in my hands. 'That's OK, honey. There'll be somewhere you can wait while Taylor and I go in.'

For once, Taylor didn't sneer at his tears. With her eyes fixed on the ground she followed me silently into the building, hovering close behind as I signed the three of us in at reception. In a rare show of solidarity, when Reece was led away by an unfamiliar social worker to sit in her office, Taylor patted him on the back.

The two of us then made our way up a set of metal stairs towards one of the conference rooms on the second floor, both lost in our own thoughts. Some childish part of me wanted to grab hold of her in the stairwell and demand to know why she had made malicious complaints. *Why would you do that?* I wanted to demand. *How is that fair?* But the grown-up in me knew that children in care sometimes fabricated allegations for all sorts of reasons: loyalty to their parents, confusion, anger, bewilderment.

Foster carers were supposed to rise above it, remain professional and, above all, keep a cool head. Besides, Taylor had not been herself all morning, not by a long chalk. She seemed nervous and I felt a sudden, overwhelming urge to put her at ease. Diminished, all trace of her former bravado was gone and so every time I looked at her, though I was still upset about the complaints, I was also gripped by unexpected pulses of sympathy.

As we entered conference room 2, my eyes were immediately drawn to a toddler, dark-haired and tearful. Momentarily confused by the sight, I realised, when Taylor gasped, that it was Bailey. He was sitting on the lap of a thick-set man who looked strangely familiar to me, though I wasn't sure why – an ex-neighbour perhaps, or someone I'd passed in the supermarket or street. Wearing a smart polo shirt and dark chinos, with a pair of sunglasses perched on the top of his broad head, it struck me that the children bore little resemblance to him and so it wasn't the family connection that I had recognised. Square was the word that sprung to mind when I looked at him, the noun sense of the word rather than the verb. Across one cheek, just below his right eye, was a deep scar, furrowed and colourless in his otherwise tanned face.

As soon as little Bailey caught sight of his sister he threw his arms out, straining to get to her. She rushed forwards. 'Hello, little pickle,' she said as she took him into her arms, her tone amazingly gentle.

Bailey's face was a picture as she walked back around the table towards me. Shiny eyed, he couldn't stop staring at her. 'This is my little brother,' she announced proudly when she reached my side, bobbing him up and down on her hip.

'Well, hello, little man,' I crooned, leaning forwards and taking his chubby little hand into my own. 'Oh, he's gorgeous, Taylor,' I told her. She beamed at me, not one of her twisted sneers but a broad, warm smile that lit up her whole face.

At that moment one of the people present cleared their throat and then several things happened at once. Mr Fielding, Taylor's father, lifted his hands and gestured for her to return Bailey to his lap, several people withdrew pens from handbags or pockets and the low whisper of conversation from the group came to an abrupt stop.

As soon as Taylor and I sat down the chairman, a Liverpudlian in his early forties with slightly protruding teeth, started to explain the purpose of a LAC review (to ensure the child's needs are being met and that there is a suitable care plan in place) and then moved on to introductions, asking each of us to introduce ourselves.

Several people were seated in a semi-circle around the large oval conference table, the empty seats between each of them suggesting that none were well acquainted. Mrs Fielding was conspicuous by her absence and when everyone had introduced themselves, Taylor nodding mutely at me when it was her turn to tell everyone who she was, the chairman, Phil Walters, explained that she was too unwell to attend.

'She's finding it difficult to cope with the kids being away,' Nick Fielding explained in a bass tone as he bobbed Bailey up and down on his knee. Since Taylor had handed the toddler back he'd been whimpering, his little bottom shivering as if he was cold. 'That's why I had to bring the little 'un here. She's a bit … fragile at the moment.' Nick's voice was soft, soothing even. It was difficult to imagine him raising his voice, let alone his fists, in domestic disputes. Taylor shuffled around in her seat, her hands restless in her lap. I got the impression that she was aching to hold her brother and comfort him, his distraught whimpers getting to her as they were to me.

Phil hesitated for a moment, staring at Nick over the top of half-moon spectacles, but then he pushed them further up his nose to survey the rest of us. 'Right, so, as Taylor has agreed to join us,' he directed a warm smile her way and she scowled in response, 'let's start with the issues that concern her. We'll move on to the boring stuff later. That OK, Taylor?'

She shrugged, her cheeks blazing red.

'OK, so how are you settling in at Rosie's house?'

She glanced at me and then shrugged again. 'Mnn-mmn-mnn,' she said, which the chairman seemed to correctly interpret as 'I don't know.'

'Let's start with your room then? You have one to yourself, don't you?'

She nodded.

'That must be nice, after sharing with your younger brother at home.'

She stared at the table. He was going to have to work harder than that.

'OK, how about Rosie's children? Are they good housemates to have? Emily and Jamie, isn't it?'

I nodded and looked at Taylor, her head so low that part of her fringe was brushing the table. 'Mnn-mmn-mnn.'

'And Rosie? How are you getting along with her?'

'Mnn-mmn-mnn,' she mumbled again, her voice strained.

'She don't like it there,' Nick said, looking at me for the first time. I met his gaze. After a moment I felt uncomfortable and glanced away, aware that he was still staring. 'My wife has been through all this with madam here,' he lifted one of his stout hands, indicating Maisie. 'The kids ain't happy there. They wanna come home.'

Bailey whimpered and Taylor looked up, her face tormented.

'So, I have to say,' Maisie said, wrapping a lacy knit cardigan around herself, 'I've visited Rosie's home and, as far as I can tell, there are no grounds for concern. The complaints themselves are low level and I'm sure it's just a case of the children needing some time to settle in.' She turned to Taylor, who was still refusing to meet anyone's eye. 'It's good that you've got the confidence to let us know when you're not happy, Taylor, but Rosie is trying hard to make you as comfortable as possible. I think it would be a good idea to give it another week or two and then we'll have another chat. How do you feel about that?'

Taylor blew out her cheeks and nodded. I couldn't help but feel sorry for her. At just ten years old, it seemed unfair to expect her to stand up in front of a room full of people and justify the complaints she had made, particularly in my presence. The poor child had turned puce with all the attention. I felt a pulse of admiration towards Maisie for the unexpected solidarity. We'd had our disagreements but she had put them aside and defended my care. I was grateful for that.

I could almost feel Taylor's relief when the conversation moved on to education. Miss Cooper, Taylor's class teacher, who sat two seats away from Nick Fielding, gave a sanitised summary of the child's progress in school, referring only briefly to Taylor's 'occasional difficulties in getting along with her peers'. Reece's class teacher was next, a young woman with a bright open smile and long ponytail, who said that the six-year-old had 'blossomed' since coming into care. Their father bristled at that and Bailey, tuned in to his mood, began whimpering again. Health was next, the rotund paediatrician detailing Taylor's injuries. 'According to the child,' Dr Frieston said, without looking up from the file in front of him, 'Taylor sustained the injuries at school.' He made it clear that he doubted the explanation and Taylor's flush deepened.

Shifting her chair a little closer to me, she clutched the rim of the conference table with her right hand, clinging on tight as if she expected a tornado to strike at any moment. The veins on the backs of her hands were swollen, visibly pulsing.

Miss Cooper looked shocked. 'At school? Is that true, Taylor?'

She nodded vigorously and then looked at me, her eyes brimming with tears. 'Can I leave now, Rosie? Please?' There was panic in her voice and with a sombre nod of affirmation from Maisie, I escorted her from the room. Shrunken out of all recognition, she sat down on one of the chairs lined up outside and dropped her face into cupped hands.

Back in the room, the tone had changed. Maisie was speaking directly to Nick and although her tone was its usual low monotone, there was a clipped edge to her words that told me she wasn't keen on him. Despite his heavy tan, I could tell that his dusky cheeks were flushed. Once again, Bailey picked on the altered pitch, his big brown eyes sweeping miserably around the room. 'Ra-ra,' he whined over and over, his long lashes glistening. I wondered whether he was calling for Taylor.

'That's not what happened,' Nick replied to whatever Maisie had said calmly, but there was an undercurrent of irritation. 'She gave him a quick slap across the leg, that's all. Reece bruises easily. Always has.'

Maisie winced at the cliché. 'I don't accept that, Mr Fielding. And however lightly you suggest the slap was, it was still unacceptable.'

'And I get that,' he said, tapping a fist gently on the top of the table. 'But she's a good mum apart from that. She makes one mistake and you do this to us. What has this country come to, eh?'

Maisie sighed. 'There are other issues here, Mr Fielding. Like your refusal to submit to psychiatric assessments. Like the fact that the police have been called to your address several times over the years, after physical fights between you and your wife.'

'Yeah, well that's the neighbours calling 'em, not us. Claire gets a bit het up, that's all. Outsiders need to learn to mind their own business.' Beads of sweat glistened on his forehead and his scar, at least two inches long and as wide as one of those chubby pencils that toddlers use, glowed even whiter. It was an effort to maintain eye contact without my gaze lingering on his cheek.

'It's the impact on the children we're concerned about. Research suggests that –'

'Christ, spare us the lecture,' he groaned, his finger chasing a trickle of sweat down the side of his face. The cleft deepened as he jutted his chin and glanced around the room. I got the feeling he was trying to canvass support. 'Oh, come *on*,' he said in response to the sombre, non-committal expressions around the table. 'You're telling me I can't have a spat with my own wife now without the Gestapo getting involved and blowing it all out of proportion? The kids are happy as Larry, don't you worry about that.'

'We have every reason to worry, Mr Fielding. And minimising the problem makes me all the more concerned.'

My own heart was racing but Maisie remained calm and in control, her gaze never leaving his face as she spoke. I felt another flare of respect towards her then and was pleased to see that it was Nick who looked away first.

The chairman eventually steered the conversation around to contact and while arrangements were being discussed, my mind began to wander. I thought about Taylor's strange metamorphosis. She struck me as a child who loved to hold court, relishing the attention of others. Had she been intimidated by her father's presence, I wondered. There had been little interaction between them, considering she had been away from home for almost a week. With his strong, square jaw and well-defined physique, Nick was good looking, if you appreciated the flashy, hard man look. With an adorable child on his lap, I hoped he was a better man than the circumstances, and the coins, suggested.

My thoughts were interrupted by a loud shriek of distress from Bailey, who seemed to be drawing little comfort from his father's hugs. 'I'm done here,' Nick said, standing and throwing Bailey roughly over his shoulder. The toddler cried out in surprise and I noticed several of those present wincing. My teeth began to grind. 'But let me tell you lot this,' he said, waggling a meaty finger around the room. 'No one splits my family up, d'you hear me? If I can't have my kids, no one's gonna have them.'

The fluorescent light overhead buzzed loudly and seemed to give his deep voice a sinister edge. Perhaps it was just me and my overactive imagination, but his words seemed to sharpen the fetid air like a frosted wind, hovering over the conference table long after he had finished speaking.

When we arrived home the lamp light outside our small wooden porch flickered on and Taylor started, jerking sideways as if she'd been struck. Maisie had leapt to her feet when Nick Fielding stormed out of the meeting, accompanying him from the building. I wasn't sure whether there had been any interaction between him and Taylor on the way out but she had been quiet and introspective in the car, barely lifting her head when I picked Emily and Jamie up.

After the meeting I had managed to speak to Maisie briefly, before Taylor joined us. She looked mystified when I began telling her about an old school friend of mine, Kim, who was a prison officer. 'Kim says that inmates are always finding new ways to smuggle contraband into the prison. They hide it under their tongue and burrow it into their skin. One of the wives even managed to smuggle heroin in to her hubby by making him hand-made cards – she'd been mixing the drug in with the paint. It was only discovered when one of the screeners noticed that the colours were always a bit murky.'

'Fascinating,' Maisie said slowly, 'but, Rosie, what's that got to do –'

'Sorry, I'll get to the point,' I had said. 'Kim said that some of the inmates, the dealers, when they're on the outside, they hide drugs inside frozen foods in case their house is raided.'

Maisie was looking at me as if I'd taken leave of my senses.

'Anyway, the reason I'm telling you all of this is ...' I took a breath. It all sounded a bit weak, now I was saying it out loud. 'Reece said that Taylor broke her tooth on a coin after eating a meal her mother had cooked.'

The social worker shook her head, looking at me from the corner of her eye. 'Rosie, I –'

'What I'm saying is that I think their mother is planning to run. That is, she's wants to leave but she can't do it the traditional way. She's trying to save money and hiding it where she thinks it won't be found. There's only one reason she'd do that – she must be scared – scared out of her wits. I don't think she's the problem, Maisie. I think it's him: Nick. He's the one doing all of this.'

Maisie gave a dismissive laugh. 'I think maybe you're reading too much into a few coins, Rosie.'

I felt myself flush. 'You should have seen Taylor's reaction when Reece said it. It was that more than anything else …'

She had looked thoughtful. 'Hmm, it's something I'll need to ask her about –' her voice lapsed as she chewed her lip. 'We can't talk about it here, but there's a case conference coming up.' The social worker went on to say that investigations were continuing and 'action would be taken in the next few days'.

As we neared home I wondered what Maisie had been hinting at when she said that action would be taken, and then my thoughts turned to little Bailey. He was one of those pudgy little boys with big melting eyes that you just wanted to scoop up and squeeze in a tight hug. The more I thought about it, the more I felt there was something disquieting in the way he looked at his sister, as if silently appealing to her from across the room.

As soon as I opened the front door Taylor went straight upstairs to her room, closing the door without slamming it, something she hadn't ever managed before. When she came down her eyes were circled with red, as if she'd taken a kohl pencil and applied liner until she'd drawn blood. I expected her to fly to the computer but she didn't even ask to use it. She hardly touched her sandwich either and as soon as lunch was over, she returned to her room, staying there for the rest of the afternoon. It was the same that evening. She ate very little and sat, morose and untouchable, on the other side of a divide.

As I made myself a warm drink that night, my thoughts were still lingering on the meeting and Taylor's strange mouse-like transformation in front of her father. Over-inquisitive though it might have been, I also couldn't stop wondering how her father came by his scar. Had Claire Fielding attacked him during one of their 'spats'? And then, with a frisson of electricity pulsing through my veins, I remembered how familiar he had seemed to me. For the life of me, though, I couldn't work out why that should be.

I replayed his parting comment at the review – 'If I can't have my kids, then no one's gonna have them.'

His words were open to interpretation, but it wasn't too much of a stretch to draw something sinister from them.

Chapter Thirteen

And so the days of the Easter holiday slipped by, each one as difficult as the last. With Taylor's sniping a constant background murmur and rows over screen time never far away, there was barely a moment when I felt at ease. Even when I was in bed I couldn't relax, the events of each day spooling through my mind on an endless loop.

That's not to say there weren't moments of triumph. Reece had plucked up the courage for a nappy amnesty, managing four dry nights in a row. The breakthrough seemed to have boosted his confidence so that, although he remained hyper-vigilant, starting at the slightest noise, his twitching had reduced, along with his largely imaginary ailments. As far as Taylor was concerned, she and Jamie seemed to have reached an understanding; his love of humour making him the perfect sounding board for Taylor's quick wit.

Working on the principle that keeping busy would chase away their worries, I made sure we had at least one trip planned each day, even if it was only a walk to the park or along the riverbank. The universal band-aid worked well, giving them less time to fret, to brood. On Easter Sunday I woke early, hiding clues to a treasure hunt all around the garden. In an effort to encourage their growing camaraderie, I split the children into teams to solve the clues, Taylor and Jamie on one side, Emily and Reece on the other. Although she loved chocolate, Emily was the least competitive child I had ever known, so it was no surprise when Taylor and Jamie won. Their childish celebration as they rolled across the grass cheering was heart warming to watch; one of those rare moments when I was reminded just how young and vulnerable Taylor was. In the next instant it was gone, replaced by a flick of her hair, a curling lip.

Despite my detailed daily diaries, I couldn't spot a pattern to her moods, although I had noticed that she became increasingly distracted, depressed even, after using the computer. 'Why do you sit and stare at that thing when it makes you so miserable?' I asked her time and time again. 'Oh for God's sake, you're such a dinosaur,' was her stock, hissed response. 'One of those sneaky flying ones with the beady little eyes. Strictly speaking you should be dead.' I had parental controls in place but, without constantly hovering at her shoulder, it was difficult to know exactly what she was accessing online. I had warned her several times of the dangers lurking in cyberspace. I suspected my advice went in one ear and out the other; she just thought of me as hopelessly out of touch.

Torn

Invariably we had some project or other on the go – one afternoon we made chocolate marshmallow krispie squares and the next a gingerbread house with strawberry laces for the front door and chocolate fingers for the eaves. I taught Reece to ride a bike without stabilisers and Taylor to macramé. She often forgot herself as we worked, chatting away about this and that but, as always, whenever I steered the conversation towards home and family she clammed up.

Her room became a real bone of contention between us. Increasingly fetid, I could barely get near her bed to change it for all the books, clothes and make-up littering the floor. Meticulous as she was with personal hygiene and grooming, the disorder struck me as strange, completely at odds with her nature. Whenever I suggested that we clean up together she flew off the handle, quoting my own words when I had assured her that her room was her own private space and I would only cross the threshold if invited.

One rainy day, towards the end of the holidays, Jamie asked if they could build an indoor camp using quilts and sheets. It was a game we had often resorted to on those endless days at home when the weather was bad and he and Emily had always enjoyed it. Since breakfast the house had grown increasingly noisy, bangs and crashes echoing off the walls as the four children tried to dispel their boredom. Feeling sorry for the neighbours, I got to work pegging blankets along the top of our tall bookshelf and over the door. Reece and Jamie crawled beneath, their giggles rebounding around the room. The girls showed no interest at first but by the time I had finished and the living room had been transformed into a giant tepee, they joined in, sectioning off a piece of territory just for themselves.

It was while they were messing around inside that I happened to knock against the desk (the only part of the room not shrouded in old sheets) on my way to the kitchen. The computer stuttered into life and so I shuffled the mouse around and clicked, preparing to close it down. As I did so the Myspace homepage filled the screen and my face immediately coloured – Taylor was logged in.

I stood for a moment, glancing over my shoulder and then back to the screen. Telling myself that it was wrong to snoop, even if my motives were honourable, I sat down on the chair intending to double click and shut down. My fingers seemed to have a mind of their own however, and within seconds, wilfully ignoring the privacy debate going on in my mind, I began scrolling down the page.

A quick look couldn't hurt, I told myself. It was up to me to supervise the children, both online and offline and I had warned Taylor several times not to use the site. The first thing I noticed was the profile picture she had chosen. Rather touchingly, it was a close-up of Taylor and Emily, heads touching, eyes half-closed in laughter. Below was the surprising caption 'Me and my Foster Sister', followed by a large red heart. Aware that Taylor was just a few feet away from me on the other side of a sheet, my heart beat a little faster as I scrolled down to read some of her latest status updates, slowly at first, but then faster and faster:

OMG!! Deffo died and gone to choco heaven!!! Feeling … happy! :-)

Torn

She was referring to our trip to the Cadbury museum and below there were comments from her friends. Some of them made no sense to my rapidly scanning eyes, the words almost unrecognisable with missing vowels and random stars where letters should be. One of them jumped out at me though, the message courtesy of someone calling themselves tellitlikeitis: *Would deffo make my day if you croaked it, darling, you're disgusting. No one can stand u, u get that, right? Why don't you do us all a favour?*

I sat back, breathing hard. There were several replies to that comment. One of them was simple enough to understand: *WTF?!* The others were indecipherable and so it was difficult to gauge whether they were condemning the suggestion or egging her on.

I was beginning to realise why she was surrounded by an air of gloom whenever she used the computer. Sickened but strangely hooked, I sat quietly for a moment to make sure one of them wasn't about to emerge from the tent, and then began scrolling down to earlier status updates.

Bagged the coolest stuff on the planet today – 6 bags not enough for my hoard!

Pinned to the update was a photo of Taylor draped over her bed, an assortment of shoes, bags and clothes arranged in front of her. The message appeared to have been uploaded on Saturday, the day she had barely moved from the computer and then had the distressing phone call with her mum. There had been no shopping trip; it had been a miserable day, and the items surrounding her seemed to be clothes she already owned, with price tags carefully positioned on top.

Some predictable replies followed: *OMG! So cool!* and *Jealous!*

And then a particularly noxious comment from honestchick: *Don't matter how much you spend, doll, you still look like a dog …*

Feeling slightly nauseous, I stared at the screen and thought about all the pressures Taylor was facing. With so many mixed messages coming at her, it wasn't surprising that she so often seemed angry and confused. I wasn't sure whether to continue reading. Part of me felt a responsibility to carry on but it was such depressing reading and suddenly I felt terribly sad. There was something tragic about a young girl fabricating the perfect life, as if what she had to offer the world was nowhere near good enough. Why did she feel the need to parade herself online anyway, when the likes of tellitlikeitis lay ready to strike? And, come to think of it, how had she managed to negotiate her way around the parental controls to access the site?

A noise from behind took the decision out of my hands. A few seconds after I had clicked on the X to close down the screen, Reece emerged from the tent. 'Rosie? Can I use your phone for a bit?'

I turned around, my cheeks pulsing pink. 'My phone? Why?'

'We want to play a game.'

I went to the kitchen drawer and dug out all the old mobile handsets. Luckily enough, there were four in total. 'Thanks!' he said, holding them to his chest and diving back into the tent. There were gleeful shouts as he handed them out to the others and a noisy, giggly game ensued. It was lovely to hear them getting on so well and I couldn't help but smile as I made myself a cup of tea and sat back in front of the blank computer screen.

I laid my head back against the chair, enjoying the rare moment of peace. Their chatter faded into a background hum, but when Reece shrieked as if he'd won a year's free Lego, my head shot up. 'Taylor! You won't believe this! I just got a text from Mum!'

There was a tiny pause and then she asked: 'What does it say?'

'It says she loves us and she's not sad no more!'

'Hooray!' Taylor cheered and the others joined in. 'And I've just got one as well,' the ten year old said a moment later, her voice happy and light. 'Basically, Mum says everything is OK now and we can go back home!'

'Wow! Taylor, we can all dance together in the kitchen like we used to. And help Mum make cakes and snuggle up together in bed!'

The fantasy texts continued for a few minutes, each one filled with promises of family days out, security and happiness. I lowered my cup to the desk and swallowed hard over the catch in my throat. That was the funny thing about caring for Taylor – there were days when she drove me almost to distraction, but then she would do or say something that seized me by the heart – compassion and frustration pulling in opposite directions until I wasn't really sure what I felt.

Chapter Fourteen

The sit-ins resumed with a vengeance on the first day back at school after the Easter holidays, getting later and later as each day passed. And even more disheartening, Miss Cooper had confided, during one painfully long sit-in I feared may never end, that Taylor was still struggling to get along with her classmates. I had hoped that some time away from the turmoil going on at home might help her to mellow, but if anything, her bullying of others had intensified.

Having seen some of the toxic messages sent to Taylor via Myspace, I knew that she had caught the attention of some particularly nasty cyber 'friends', but something told me they were teenagers, or even adults, not classmates. The story she span about her injuries never really rang true with me and so, while I knew she had few friends, I hadn't quite realised the extent of the problems she was having with her own peers.

The sad truth was that children viewed everyone in their lives through the prism of their past. Consequently, the only way Taylor knew how to relate to anyone was by using physical force and harsh words. It wasn't unusual for her to be the only one in the class without a party invite and she would often come home and break her heart over the rejection. Given the loud, uncompromising timbre of her voice and her overriding air of confidence, no one would ever have guessed at the fragility beneath. It sometimes even caught me by surprise.

At the end of the third week back at school, towards the end of May, we were still in the classroom at quarter past six. The sit-in came as a surprise; it was the first time she had refused to leave school in days. That was the way it was with Taylor – just when I thought I had a problem licked, up it popped again, with no apparent trigger. Emily, Jamie and Reece were all lying on their tummies on a large rug in the corner of the classroom, their heads together. On the floor in front of them was a piece of paper on which they were playing noughts and crosses, but what had begun as neat squares with carefully drawn digits was turning into angry scrawl. They had had enough, and so, it seemed, had Miss Cooper. Her usual high, bouncy ponytail was looking decidedly lacklustre, her cheeks crimson with frustration.

Striding over to Taylor, who was leaning back in her chair with her knees touching the desk in front of her, she cleared her throat. 'Taylor, that's it now. We're going. If you don't come we'll leave you here on your own.'

Taylor didn't move, not even to lift her head.

'Taylor!' Miss Cooper snapped, raising her voice as if there was a chance that Taylor hadn't heard her. 'I said we're going!' The teacher's eyes flicked from her pupil to the door, somewhat panicked. Usually placatory, she really had reached her limit and I couldn't blame her. Taylor had never held on for so long before and I was beginning to wonder myself how much more we could all take. It wasn't as much a problem for me – I was pretty certain that Taylor found the whole exercise more boring than I did, but it wasn't at all fair on the other children.

I had racked my brain trying to find a solution, but absolutely nothing seemed to work. Personally, I was convinced that ignoring her was the best policy and had voiced my feelings privately to Miss Cooper. She had agreed, but didn't seem able to follow through with the desired level of feigned nonchalance. Now, she sucked her cheeks in and clapped her hands. 'Right, get up!' she shrieked, flattened hand rising through the air, palm upwards, like a rookie magician trying her luck at levitation.

Taylor turned her head minutely, blinked once, then fixed her stare back on the whiteboard at the front of the class.

'We're going then!' Miss Cooper yelled, as one might to a stubborn toddler. She shuffled backwards towards the door, but it was a futile threat and Taylor knew it. She was confident that we wouldn't leave her behind – that was the beauty of her protest. All of us were all splayed, headfirst, over the proverbial barrel.

The tiniest shrug of Taylor's shoulders yielded a cry of frustration from Miss Cooper. The ten-year-old flinched slightly when her teacher sank down on her chair in defeat, almost as if she regretted her own behaviour. Maybe it was brain fog due to tiredness, or perhaps because I had one final trick up my sleeve, but seeing someone else struggling with Taylor actually tickled me that day. Suppressing a wayward grin, I chided myself for being so uncharitable. 'How about you go to the staffroom and have a cuppa, Miss Cooper,' I said calmly. 'I'll text you when we're ready to leave.'

With Miss Cooper out of the room and one less person to play up to, the sit-in came to an end soon afterwards. The children were all unusually quiet as they secured their seatbelts in the car. Overtired and hungry, even Taylor had little to say. Energised by the prospect of playing my trump card, my own fatigue lifted as soon as I turned the ignition. Humming softly as we headed towards home, I glanced in the rear-view mirror and felt a flicker of satisfaction at the look of bemusement on Taylor's face.

'Hey, Mum, thanks!' Jamie cheered as I pulled into the drive-in of a fast-food restaurant. 'We're getting take-out!' he announced joyfully to the others, in an American sing-song accent. Taylor's face lit up and a chorus of cheers went around the car. My pulse picked up a little. Bracing myself for the fall-out, I asked everyone what they would like. Taylor, not surprisingly, was the first to shout. 'I'll have the large chicken meal with fries and –'

'Ah, Taylor,' I said, forcing a level tone, 'I told you last week that if you refused to leave school on time again you'd lose all of your privileges for a whole day. Do you remember?'

She glowered at me. 'Yeah, but food ain't a privilege.' She spoke in a superior tone, with a firm nod of her head, as if that settled the matter and I should get on with ordering. 'It's like air and water. It's a human right.'

Inching towards the kiosk behind another car, I held her gaze in the mirror. 'Of course it is, and I have a casserole in the oven at home. It'll be ready for you as soon as we get in.'

Her jaw dropped. 'You can't do that!' she shrieked. 'That ain't fair!'

Remembering something Des had told me about fairness, I felt a moment's self-doubt. Apparently, social workers had conducted an extensive study to try and find out what looked-after children valued most in the foster home. Almost unanimously, the children had chosen fairness as being most important. I paused. Was I being unfair? She was absolutely livid and I didn't feel altogether comfortable with leaving her out. 'I gave you enough warnings, Taylor,' I said, having convinced myself that something had to be done. 'Takeaway food is a treat and you certainly don't deserve that.'

Spitting feathers, my mother would call it. As I rolled off our order into the microphone, Taylor sat in the back, her face a deep shade of crimson. I knew it was likely that she would make a complaint to Maisie, and I was also pretty certain that the social worker wouldn't support my actions. But I had given the softly, softly approach a fair chance and it had completely and utterly failed. For everyone's sake, including Taylor's, she needed to learn that the feelings of others should be considered, as well as her own, even if that meant learning the hard way. Driving home, I felt more in control than I had since the siblings first arrived. In my mind I had turned a corner. Whether that translated into reality remained to be seen.

Taking the idea of considering the feelings of others one step further, I invited Taylor to play a game with me the following morning. Still mourning the loss of her chicken burger but ever so slightly intrigued, she sulkily left the computer and followed me into the garden, barking at the others to stay inside.

Seated on a chair at the patio table, she was watching me expectantly, though the usual sneer remained in position on her face. 'There's a girl about your age called Josie. She lives a few miles from here,' I said, leaning my arms on the table and interlacing my fingers.

'So what?'

'So, her mother left home when she was young, and now she's living alone with her dad.'

Taylor shrugged. 'And?' she asked. 'What do I care?' But her eyes were shining with curiosity. Children in care seemed to love hearing about others living in extremis. I could tell that Taylor wanted to know more.

'She's lonely,' I said, keeping my eyes focussed on my hands. 'And that makes her sad.'

'Why don't she make some friends then?'

'She's tried. But she's shy. And she spends most of the time when she's not at school cooking and cleaning because her dad is out at work.'

'S'er fault if she's shy,' Taylor said, shrugging. 'Anyway, I thought we was gonna play a game.'

'Well, we are. The idea of the game is to come up with solutions. So we need to think of a way to help Josie, a plan to make her life better.'

'Oh, for God's sake,' she groaned rubbing her face with her hands. 'So this Josie person isn't even real?'

I shook my head, smiling. She rolled her eyes. But, to her credit, she went along with it, telling me that Josie should ask a teacher for help. She then took her turn, and of course, her example was a lot more disturbing than mine. 'Ah, I've never heard of anyone being so hungry that they had to eat floorboards before,' I said, when she'd finished telling her own story. Not surprisingly, it had been a fairly bloodthirsty one.

She laughed out loud, enjoying the game, in spite of herself. 'Come on then. Come up with a solution to that!'

We played the same game regularly, at Taylor's request. The awful, alternative universe situations she managed to dream up were truly terrible to hear but we always ended the game with strategies for helping 'Alex who had lost his entire family and was sleeping rough inside a large rat-infested drain' or the teenager who was made to drink bleach by her drug-addled parents. By imagining what it must be like for others who experience hardship, I hoped to encourage Taylor to see things from their point of view.

That's not to say that there wasn't already a generous amount of kindness in her. She kept it well hidden but some-times it would manifest itself when I least expected it. Later that afternoon, for example, as I stood drenched in the kitchen with pools of water at my feet, Taylor sprang into action, doing her best to help. I had been trying to unblock the sink and managed to crack one of the water pipes instead. Temporarily helpless, I hopped from foot to foot in the middle of the kitchen, making silly, desperate screechy noises.

'Where's the stop-cock?!' she shouted above the chaos, the other children staring at me in surprise. 'You need to turn the water off at the mains.'

'Oh goodness, I have no idea.' I had rented the house we were living in after separating from Gary and hadn't even thought to find out such a detail.

'It'll be under here somewhere,' she said, rummaging around in the kitchen cupboards despite the jets of water spraying all over the place. After a moment I joined her in the search, amazed at her practicality. But then, as we scoured the kitchen it occurred to me; of course she was practical – with a deeply depressed mother at home she'd probably had little choice but to find ways of coping. She managed to find the stop-cock first and together, giggling breathlessly, we turned the water off.

Afterwards, she searched online to find the number for a local emergency plumber, even sorting out one with a reasonable call-out charge. When the plumber had left and we were all dry, Taylor was in a buoyant mood, and when I thanked her for helping she beamed, her habitual scowl nowhere to be seen. I wasn't sure how long it would last. Until about tea-time as it turned out.

* * *

'Where's Taylor?' I asked the others at about quarter to six. Dinner was almost ready and, since she had been in a helpful mood, I was going to ask her to set the table outside on the patio.

'Dunno,' Reece said, looking up from his book. 'I think I heard her in your room earlier.'

'*My* room?' I said, already halfway there. The last time I'd checked she had been sitting at the computer, staring intently. Taylor knew that my bedroom was out of bounds, even though it had once been a dining room. Discomfort mounted in my chest as I crossed the hall, my eyes fixed on the door which was slightly ajar. Alarm bells were already ringing in my head as I flung it open and when my eyes adjusted to the scene in front of me my stomach lurched. Standing utterly still, I almost cried out in horror. My wardrobe doors were open and in front of them several boxes had been tipped over onto their sides. Spread across the floor were my photo albums, upended, as if they'd been thrown, their contents torn into tiny pieces. I stood unmoving, my hand covering my mouth.

'Taylor!' I shouted, when I'd finally found my voice.

Emily, Jamie and Reece were at my side within moments, Emily gasping when she peered over my shoulder. 'Oh no!' she squealed. She loved looking through all of our old photos. It was something we did every now and again, snuggled together on the sofa with a duvet across our laps.

A dull thud sounded distantly and, furious, I left the three of them staring open mouthed at the mess and charged upstairs, my pulse racing. Feeling sick as I approached her room, I clenched my shaking hands into fists and rapped on her door in a rapid series of knocks. 'Why would you do that?' I snapped after bursting into her room. My innards were trembling. The sit-ins, the answering back, the defiance, all got to me but this, this felt deeply personal. 'Why?'

She was already crying. 'I don't know,' she wailed, her bottom lip quavering. 'I'm sorry, Rosie.'

Of all the reactions, I hadn't expected that. Like much of her behaviour, it was bizarre, impossible to rationalise, and beneath my anger I felt strangely protective of her.

'What do you mean, you don't know?' I demanded, colour bleeding into my cheeks with the effort of holding back tears. 'You've destroyed something that can never be replaced.' I was so upset that I couldn't stop my voice from cracking, although, in truth, my mum and Gary had copies of some of the photos, at least that was what I hoped. But it was still upsetting. Some of the pictures were irreplaceable and therefore priceless, to me at least.

She looked mortified, certainly too ashamed to meet my eyes. 'I know. I don't know why I did it. I'm sorry.' She was sobbing and her eyes were pleading with me but I was so hurt, so furious, that I turned my back on her and slammed the door behind me.

Downhearted and battle-weary, I could never have dreamed that night, as I climbed exhausted into my bed, that within twenty-four hours Taylor would up her game.

Chapter Fifteen

Still grieving over the loss of my photos the next morning as I made myself an early cup of coffee, I began chanting a mantra, over and over in my head. *I will do better. I can do better. We all deserve better.* Sipping at my drink as I left the kitchen, I pictured myself nodding serenely as Taylor stomped and shouted her way through the day. In my comfortable wicker chair beside the patio doors with the early morning sun streaming through the windows, it was easy to convince myself that today would be the day when, with Herculean effort, I would harmonise our interactions and turn our pattern of 'one step forwards, two steps back' on its head.

A distant boom on the stairs sent my pulse racing, a Pavlovian response to Taylor's imminent arrival. No child is unreachable, I told myself, but at the sight of the ten-year-old crossing the hall, elbows pumping, face screwed up in an angry scowl, I felt my good intentions slipping out of reach. 'Morning, Taylor,' I said brightly, going to the fridge to pour her a glass of milk. 'What's up?'

'Ask him!' she shrieked, gesturing towards the door with her chin. It appeared that her guilt over the ruined photos was well and truly gone.

Reece arrived at the threshold, his eyes pooling with tears. My heart sank. 'What's the matter, sweetie?'

'I got my finger stuck in the drawer,' he said tearfully, 'but *she* wouldn't help me and you couldn't hear me calling you.'

'Yeah and he was carrying on so much he woke me up.'

'Oh, darling, I'm sorry.' I lifted his finger to the light and then gave it a rub. There wasn't a mark to be seen but his pain threshold was low, bless him. 'Taylor, help your brother next time, OK?' I said in a measured tone as I drew Reece into a hug.

She stared at me impassively. 'Taylor, honey?'

'Why should I? It's not me being paid to look after him is it? You're the one getting all the dosh.'

'Taylor,' I said warningly, 'do you want to lose even more screen time?' But she just rolled her eyes at me.

The argument between Taylor and Reece continued throughout the school run, and in the rear-view mirror I could see their clandestine attempts to whack each other. 'That's enough!' I yelled, deducting yet another ten minutes from their screen time. The punishment was futile, since Taylor was already three hours in the red, but stuck behind the wheel of the car, there wasn't a whole lot else I could do.

It was another one of those times when I felt immensely grateful to Emily and Jamie. They weren't perfect children by any stretch of the imagination, but they possessed an amazing ability to rise above everyday angst. Despite all that was going on around them, Emily was staring serenely out of the window and every now and again Jamie would pipe up with something of interest, raising his voice over the argument as if it were merely inconvenient background noise.

A major turning point came just before lunchtime that day when, armed with rubber gloves and some disinfectant, I went upstairs to clean the bedrooms. I had warned Taylor for days that if she didn't do something about the assorted piles of junk and fetid smell, I would have to break our agreement and clean her room myself. When we arrived home from her latest sit-in, I gave her an absolute final warning, but she had merely shrugged, disbelieving.

I decided to tackle Reece's room first since, of all the children, his was the neatest. I piled his toy boxes up at the end of his bed, vacuumed the carpet and turned back his duvet. I was about to plump up his pillows when I caught sight of a single sheet of paper tucked beneath them. 'To Daddy,' it read, in sloping letters, some huge and others so tiny I could hardly make them out. 'I miss you. If we promise to be good and never make you angry again please can we –' and then it stopped, probably because it had taken so long for him to get the words onto the page. My heart lurched. It was so easy to forget that, however irresponsible or abusive foster carers may consider parents to be, their children still love them. Being away from home may have been keeping Reece safe from harm, but it was also making him sad.

In Taylor's room the air smelt damp and there was an undercurrent of something sharply stale. The carpet was only visible in places, the rest of the space covered in tangles of clothes and plastic toys she had collected from trips to McDonald's with her mum. And I'm the one who feeds them with junk, I thought acerbically, as I picked them up and threw them into a washing basket, along with her dirty clothes.

Some of the clothes clearly hadn't been worn and one or two items even had the tags still attached. Folding the least creased jumpers and tops carefully, I knelt on the floor and was about to lay them in the drawer at the bottom of her wardrobe when I caught another whiff of something acidic. Putting the clothes to one side, I lifted the lavender-infused paper lining in the drawer and checked between the piles of clothes already there. Nothing. But the smell was intensifying, almost overpowering.

Rising slowly, I wrinkled my nose and sniffed again, almost retching this time. It occurred to me then that the wardrobe, indeed the whole room, smelt like the neglected changing room in an old swimming baths. Certain that something was disturbingly wrong as I pulled the doors of her wardrobe open, my stomach began to roll. The rail at the top was so crammed full of hangers that it was difficult to move the clothes along but when I did, I noticed a number of plastic bottles arranged in an untidy pile on the base above the drawer.

My hand reached out, automatically, to grab one of the bottles. I held it up at eye level, noticing for the first time the yellowy brown liquid inside. Squinting, I saw that it had thickened and was crusting at the edges. At that moment my mind identified the smell – it was ammonia. Taylor, for some unfathomable reason, had been stockpiling her own urine. Flinging the bottle back on the shelf with a yelp, I scrambled from the room, panting in the same way Emily did whenever she set eyes on a spider.

It took a lot of psyching up before I was able to go back in the room and empty the wardrobe of those disgusting bottles; a task I felt really was above and beyond the call of duty. Holding the black bag at arm's length, I turned my head to the side and jogged downstairs, my face screwed up and my breath held. Pulling the front door open, I threw the bag into the wheelie bin outside and then ran to the bathroom, gasping for air. I washed my hands several times, all the while making that strange whimpering sound in my throat and dancing from foot to foot, as if the bathroom floor were covered in hot coals.

Why would *anyone* do that, I kept asking myself as I went downstairs to look for my mobile phone. Every night Taylor, like the others, had taken a plastic bottle of water up to bed with her, but it had never occurred to me that hers never came back down again.

Sucking on a mint to try and ease the churning in my stomach, I sighed with relief when my supervising social worker answered her phone. 'I'm really sorry, Karron, but you did say to call if I needed support.'

'I'm there,' she said briskly, hanging up without even asking me to expand. Within twenty minutes she was on my doorstep, calm and businesslike. 'I'll put in an urgent request for some professional help,' she said when we reached the kitchen, resting her hand on my arm. 'We'll get this thing licked, OK?'

Immediately I felt better. Karron really was the embodiment of everything a great social worker should be: worldly-wise, approachable and willing to go the extra mile to support her foster carers. Without her, my fostering years may have been cut exceedingly short.

Chapter Sixteen

The pile of out-of-date magazines, dog-eared toys and posters with frayed edges gave the impression of a doctor's waiting room. My stomach responded with twinges of anxiety, as if I was about to endure a particularly unpleasant procedure. It's just a routine chat, I kept telling myself. Part of me was longing for guidance but if I'm honest I was reluctant to reveal just how much I was struggling with the placement. Wasn't that tantamount to admitting I couldn't cope? Privately, I had come to terms with my own limitations; I really didn't want to do it in front of an audience. Since an early age I had been drawn towards fostering; it was all I really wanted to do. I certainly didn't want my employers to think that I wasn't up to the task. Trying not to think about it, I glanced around the room.

One of the posters on the wall featured a woman resting her head against a door jamb, face angled to allow observers a glimpse of her stricken expression. Her mouth was gagged with a dirty rag and emblazoned across her chest were the words: 'Abusive partner? Don't suffer in silence – HELP *is* out there.' On another, a little girl peered out from her hiding place behind a curtain, a teddy clasped to her chest. Appealing to her faceless audience with mournful, soft brown eyes, the caption beneath her read: 'Think they don't know what's going on? Peep behind the curtain and think again.'

I was wondering, absent-mindedly, how many people might have taken the brave leap of reaching out for help after reading one of those posters, when Camilla put her head around the door of her office. 'Rosie,' she said, smiling. 'Ready for you now.' I had met the psychologist once before, on one of the training courses she was facilitating. She was one of those people with an intuitive nature and knowing eyes.

Swallowing down another wisp of anxiety, I stood up quickly and followed her into a brightly lit room. Encircled in the middle of the space by four, comfortable-looking armchairs was a low coffee table, a jug of water and several glass tumblers set on top. Bookshelves stretched across the length of one wall and on the opposite side there was a wide expanse of glass, a large playroom on the other side.

'Please, sit down.' Camilla indicated one of the chairs with a gentle sweep of her arm. Tall and slim, the psychologist was dressed comfortably in black, slightly flared trousers, a plain white top and flat ballet-style shoes. Her hair, blonde and short with a slight wave, was the perfect frame for her elfin features and wide, piercing eyes. She gave the impression of sharp efficiency but there was something homely about her too; it was easy to imagine her kneeling on the floor in play sessions, gaining the trust of troubled children.

I sank down into the chair opposite her, crossed my legs and folded my arms. And then, aware of my body language, I unravelled myself and laid my hands softly in my lap. 'So, Rosie, how have things been?'

I took a deep breath. 'Erm, fairly challenging,' I said, toning down reality somewhat.

Camilla snorted. 'I'm not surprised! Four young children in one house? That's a handful for anyone, I'd say.' She leaned forward then peered theatrically towards the door. 'I'm not sure I could do it. I wouldn't have the patience.'

The knots that had bound themselves around my insides loosened a little. I settled back into my chair and grinned. 'If patience grows when you use it, I suspect that I've built up quite a stash over the past few weeks.'

Camilla laughed, an open, throaty sound that made me feel as if we were sitting in a comfortable living room somewhere, idly passing time. 'So, what would you say has been the biggest challenge?' She opened the file on her lap and flicked through the uppermost pages. I glanced around the room, wondering where to start. 'Tell you what,' she said helpfully, 'let's start with Reece. He's five, isn't he?'

'Six now,' I said. 'It was his birthday a few days after he arrived.'

Camilla nodded, smiled encouragingly. She pulled a blank sheet of lined A4 paper from the file and waited patiently, her pen poised near the top margin.

'On the whole he seems OK,' I began. 'That is, I think he's settling. He certainly seems less anxious than when he first arrived, although he still jumps around like a nervous kitten at the slightest noise.' I glanced around the room again. 'Erm, what else? It's difficult to persuade him to go to school, although he copes well once he gets there. He always seems to have a headache or tummy ache. I don't think there's been a single day when he's felt well, come to think of it. He's recently become dry at night though –' Camilla made a fist with her left hand and jabbed at the air in a gesture of triumph. I smiled. 'Yes, he was so proud of himself, bless him. I think that was a big boost to his confidence.'

Camilla nodded. 'I expect so. Being in nappies at school age can be very damaging to a child's self-esteem. I'm so pleased he's managed such an achievement, and in a relatively short space of time. That says a lot about the way he's settled. He must be feeling safe now.'

'Yes, I hope so.'

She looked thoughtful for a moment. 'In terms of anxiety, Reece's nervous system is probably all over the place. I understand there's been a long history of domestic violence in the home and children from that sort of environment are often highly strung, their brains attuned to anticipating sudden threats. I suspect it'll take a while for his emotional thermostat to regulate itself. Sadly, he may always have a low tolerance to stress, after what he's been through.'

I nodded grimly.

'School seems pleased with his progress though. It's fortunate that he's managed to keep up with his work, despite frequent absences. Children from volatile homes will often do anything to avoid going to school; desperate as they usually are to stay at home and protect their vulnerable parent. Just keep up the encouragement, Rosie. Gradually he'll learn to be a child again.'

I dipped my head. 'Yes, he's a bright boy. I find that he's dominated by Taylor somewhat, but then' – Camilla stopped writing and looked up at the mention of Taylor's name, so I gave her a wry grimace – 'we all are, to some degree.'

Camilla lifted the pen to her mouth, tapped it thoughtfully against her lips. 'Yes, Taylor. What's going on with her?'

I took a breath, straightened my back. 'Goodness, where to start?'

She held the ends of the biro, one in each hand and twirled it slowly in front of her as if roasting meat on a spit. 'How about you tell me about a typical day? Give me an idea of how you and she interact.'

I blew out my cheeks. 'Well, the day starts with a battle and ends in outright war.' I looked at the psychologist, trying to gauge her reaction. She nodded mildly so I continued, telling her about Taylor's aggressive, overbearing attitude, the sniping, the obsession with cyberspace, her increasingly messy room and the stock-piled urine, the tantrums and, finally, the sit-ins. Camilla's pen, which had been scurrying across the page, came to an abrupt halt at the mention of the last problem. She lifted her head, eyebrows raised, as if that level of creativity wasn't something she had heard of before. 'No matter what I do, nothing ever seems to please her,' I continued. 'We've been swimming, bowling, to the cinema. We went all the way down to London for the day. I've taken them to the chocolate factory because Taylor's class had been reading Roald Dahl and I thought she might feel it was a personal treat, just for her. I think she sees any trip out as a punishment, because what she'd really prefer to do is sit and stare at a screen.'

I fell silent and Camilla tapped the pen on her chin. She was quiet for a minute or so and then she tilted her head as if about to sympathise: 'It almost sounds as if you expect her to be grateful.'

Wrong footed, I dropped my head. It was a response I hadn't expected and I didn't know how to counter it. I remembered Des telling me about a couple who had adopted a young girl at the age of seven. As her social worker, Des visited soon after the adoption had been finalised to make sure that the child was settling in. The child confided that whenever her adoptive father was unhappy with her behaviour he would tell her that no one else had wanted her and she should 'think herself lucky' that she had a roof over her head, as if she should have been grateful for the rough hand that life had dealt her. My heart squeezed at the thought of it. Taylor hadn't wanted to end up at my door. Did I expect her to be grateful? I didn't think so, not at all.

When I eventually looked up, Camilla was wearing a half-smile, her expression softer than I had expected. I was mortified to find that the sight brought a lump to my throat. 'It's not as if I want thanks or anything like that,' I said, my voice high and tight. I swallowed hard and carried on. 'I just thought that if we did lots of nice things it might' – I was going to say that I thought it might help her to like me a little but I swallowed the words down, as they sounded childish and pathetic even in my own mind – 'help her to settle. And to see that there's a whole world out there to explore. I want her to appreciate real life, real people, not just those she meets online.' I paused and then added: 'And I want to try and improve our relationship. At the moment, well, it's not working too well.'

Camilla nodded, the curve of a smile touching her lips. 'Rosie, I was being deliberately provocative. Of course you're going to feel that way. But, you know, Taylor has lost everything. Her parents, her home, everything that she holds dear. I wouldn't be surprised if she thinks that you'll be taken away from her too, eventually. And she'd be right in thinking that, wouldn't she?'

I looked up slowly. 'I hadn't looked at it like that,' I said, still feeling choked. Could that be the reason she tried so hard to keep her distance? The thought hadn't occurred to me before.

Camilla paused, letting her words sink in.

'Poor Taylor,' I said softly, after a few moments. 'Nothing I do can make up for all of that.'

Camilla tilted her head one way and then the other. 'Hmm, probably not entirely. But building a strong relationship with you will help her to cope with the stress that lies ahead. Please don't get me wrong. I'm not implying that the way she's behaving is acceptable – it most certainly isn't and you shouldn't have to put up with it. What I *am* saying is that it's understandable that she wants to retreat from real life, and her activity in the virtual world is perhaps her way of doing that. She's being rewarded for it too – every time she goes online her body releases dopamine, a neurochemical that rewards the pleasure centre of the brain. It's an addiction like any other – you wouldn't believe the number of clients I have whose children are addicted to the web, or gaming, or their phones. It's a growing problem but there are effective ways of dealing with it. We'll move on to management in a moment, but first let me say that the single most powerful weapon a foster carer has in their arsenal is love.'

I nodded soberly and stared into my lap, the tension building inside my chest with the realisation that I was at fault. Where was the love I was supposed to feel for troubled children? Taylor deserved better. I felt like a complete failure.

Camilla must have noticed the shadow passing across my face. After a few moments she said, 'Can I ask you, Rosie, how you feel about Taylor?'

I looked up sharply, surprised by the question. And then my mind started freewheeling, frantically trying to focus on Taylor's charms. It wasn't as if there weren't lots to choose from. There were problems, certainly, but they didn't define her. Vivacious, single-minded, even enchanting, when she wanted to be, Taylor had a lot going for her – it's just that I couldn't think of anything pleasant that was ever directed my way. Camilla waited. 'Please, speak freely,' she urged after a few moments. 'I'm not here to judge you, Rosie. I want to try and help.'

My lips went dry. I swallowed and turned my hands over and back in my lap, staring down at them as I spoke. 'Well, I know it sounds awful to say it' – I paused, took a breath – 'but I don't like her very much.' It was a relief to find, when I glanced up, that Camilla was still smiling faintly. It was the answer she had expected all along.

'And how does that make you feel?'

That was an easy question and I answered immediately. 'Dreadful. Absolutely terrible. She's just a child and she's been through so much. I'm supposed to be helping her, but at the moment I can't seem to see past the bad stuff. If I'm really honest, my back goes up as soon as she walks into the room.'

Once again I was relieved by Camilla's reaction. She didn't gasp and proclaim that I shouldn't really be a foster carer if I didn't like children. She simply nodded knowingly and made tiny, encouraging noises in her throat.

When it was clear I wasn't going to continue she said: 'Children with traumatic pasts often thrive on pushing all the wrong buttons. They're usually very good at it too; highly skilled at assessing people and their moods because they've had to do that to survive. We call it passive aggression; deriving pleasure from taking others to the extremes of emotion. Injured souls revel in it but do you know what?'

I shook my head and waited.

'What they're really desperate to do is retain some control. When it feels as if their world is collapsing, kicking out is a natural instinct of survival.'

I tilted my head, unconvinced. 'Yes I can see that, to a degree. But to be honest, Camilla, there's nothing passive about Taylor's aggression. It's right up here,' I lifted a flat palm to my nose, 'impossible to ignore.'

She smiled. 'Yes, I see what you're saying and you're right. Aggression takes many forms, none of which are mutually exclusive. Many people overlap but one thing remains true – anger is so much easier to express than vulnerability.'

My gaze drifted to the books lining the shelves and the assortment of thank you cards pinned to a notice board across the room. There was so much to take in; so much I wished I'd known before the placement began.

'We all move from day to day hiding so much from each other, even in the closest of families. One thing is for sure though, Rosie. What you're feeling won't go away without enormous effort on your part. It will fester and grow and you'll become more and more resentful. When children are determined to make themselves unlovable there's only one thing you can really do.'

I looked back at Camilla. 'Fake it,' I said, more as a statement than a question.

She nodded. 'Absolutely. And sometimes you have to act your backside off.'

I laughed out loud. I hadn't expected someone as qualified as Camilla to be so down to earth.

Camilla chuckled then quickly grew serious. 'It's difficult to foster genuine affection for someone who rejects you, of course it is, especially when you're trying so hard to help them. All you can do to get through it is draw on the love you have for your job. The way I see it is this.' She made a steeple with her fingers and tapped her index fingers lightly on her nose. 'If a child feels something for a trusted adult they'll want to please them; that's a given, almost without exception. Call it what you will – affection, respect, fondness – but without that feeling there, it doesn't matter what you threaten to do or how stressed you get, you're never going to get anywhere with her.

'When you think about it, Taylor has already lost the most important things in her life. Why should she care if her room is a mess and you get upset over it? Leaving her personal space in a state is a way of conveying the message that her life is a mess, do you see? It reflects the way she's feeling inside. Of all the children I meet, those from violent homes can be the most difficult to unpick because their lives have depended on holding it all together, and I mean that literally.

'At the moment Taylor is wearing her aggression as a mask, insulating herself behind a ring of steel but I can guarantee you something – shrivelled up deep inside is a frightened child desperately trying to keep all the bad stuff contained. Don't forget, that young girl has learnt that vulnerability is disastrous. It's our job to teach her that it's safe to open up and show how much she's hurting inside. At the moment, all of you are living under the tyranny of her past, as often happens in foster families. It's time to take control and break the cycle, Rosie. Tell you what – try offering her a cuddle. Not when it's just the two of you alone, obviously – you have to protect yourself against allegations. But when you're around other people, give it a try and see what happens.'

My eyes widened. Had she taken leave of her senses? I couldn't imagine doing that, not for a second.

Camilla laughed. 'Daunted?'

'Absolutely! It's funny but with previous placements I've tried to guard against becoming too close. Never in a million years did I think I'd have the opposite problem.'

'It's common with older children, believe me. What *I'm* saying is that if you start to think of your relationship in terms of a bank, you'll see that you need to deposit something before you can withdraw. By injecting some warmth into your relationship, you'll qualify to take something back out. Does that make sense?'

I cupped my cheeks in my hands. 'Yes, absolutely. I know you're right. But I just can't see that happening. Taylor doesn't want anything to do with me. She certainly wouldn't want me to give her a hug!' I stared around the room, trying to find the words to explain how it really was. 'It's' – I licked my lips – 'as if she can't stand the sight of me.'

Camilla gave me a sceptical look and began flicking through the papers on her lap again. 'I've been gathering information from various agencies, as we do when we accept a child for counselling, and I've received a report from Taylor's school. They've mentioned that there have been difficulties, and I take it they're referring to these so called "sit-ins", but you may be surprised to hear that they've also noticed a huge change in her attitude since she's been staying with you.'

I frowned. Miss Cooper had mentioned problems with bullying, but I certainly hadn't heard any good reports about her. Then again, had there really been a chance?

'It sounds to me as if you're doing marvellously well, Rosie. Taylor's teacher reports that although she's still rough with her peers, she's engaging more than ever before in class. She's showing an interest in reading and is less disruptive in lessons. But best of all, she's been smiling randomly. For absolutely no reason. Isn't that marvellous? That's something that hasn't happened very often in the – oh, Rosie –'

I fumbled in my handbag for a tissue then dabbed my eyes. 'Sorry,' I said, sniffing.

She waved the apology away. 'Don't worry about it. No one has *ever* left this office with dry eyes, not one single person.' She raised her eyebrows in a mischievous arch. 'I'm rather proud of my record actually. I suppose I should have warned you about it when you came in.'

I choked a laugh into my tissue. 'I'm glad you didn't,' I said, my voice thick with emotion.

Camilla grinned then returned her attention to the report on her lap. 'Taylor often talks about you and your family, so her teacher says. Her school diary is full of what she's been up to and where she's been. So however bad things may seem to you, believe me when I say you *are* making progress, but you can't undo ten years of terror with a few kind words and day trips. Some children, particularly girls, turn their pain in on themselves, resulting in behaviours such as anorexia or self-harming. It sounds to me as if Taylor is trying her best to direct all of the anger she feels outwards. It's going to take time to overwrite something like that.'

I blew my nose, bunched the tissue up in my hand. Viewed from the dispassionate angle of an outsider, I supposed that it was easier to pick out the subtle improvements in behaviour that were lost on someone with a point-blank perspective.

'And in terms of screen-time battles, I presume you have limits in place?'

I nodded. 'Official advice seems to be no more than two hours a day, but it's a nightmare trying to get her to stick to that. I'm hoping that she'll come to appreciate what the real world has to offer but' – I twisted my lip – 'we're not there yet.'

'Be consistent. Addiction to screens becomes hardwired into the brain, altering its chemistry, so you'll need to be persistent. But it's important to stick with it, however much she rails against you. Too much screen time can cause all sorts of problems, mental and physical. Increased anxiety, depression, sleep disruption,' Camilla said, ticking each one off by tapping her pen into the palm of her other hand, 'even a lowered immunity to illnesses. I advise my clients to ban gadgets in their child's bedroom and never eat in front of the television. No phones at the table, stick to strict limits and, above all, be a good role model. Don't text your friends while your child is trying to talk to you.' Camilla raised her hand. 'Not that I'm suggesting you do that,' she smiled. 'But it's a common problem and I suspect we're going to see more and more of it as time goes on.' I noticed the psychologist's eyes drift to the clock on her desk. We had overrun by twenty minutes. 'Rosie, I'm conscious of the time so, practically speaking, I think the first step in recalibrating your relationship with Taylor is to arrange an outing for the both of you.'

'I've tried that. We already do lots together.'

'I know you do but I mean just you and Taylor. Carve out some time when no one else is around. Listen, I know it's not easy when you've got a houseful but, believe me, it will pay dividends in the long run.' Camilla spoke with the conviction of a woman who had seen it all, over the years. It was almost impossible not to trust her.

'O-K,' I said slowly. 'I'll give anything a try.'

'Great!' She tapped her biro gently on her thigh and then rose to her feet. 'Right, well, it's been lovely meeting you again, Rosie. I hope you feel it's been of some use?'

Torn

'Absolutely,' I said sincerely. I knew that the air between Taylor and I would probably still crackle with hostility when I got home, but by reassuring me that I was on the right path, Camilla had bolstered my confidence in my ability to cope. I drove towards my mother's house with a feeling of quiet determination, ready to restack the odds in my favour.

Chapter Seventeen

When I made the suggestion to Taylor the next day, it was as if I'd invited her for a tour of our nearest abattoir. After staring at me agog for a full half minute, she repeated what I'd said, as if she hadn't quite heard me correctly.

'Yes, just you and me. Reece is at his friend's house on Saturday, so we can do whatever you like, it's your choice.' Emily and Jamie were spending the weekend with my mum, an offer she had made so that they wouldn't feel left out. Still wary, Taylor nodded slowly and told me she would think about what she'd like to do. I think she wondered what she'd done to deserve such a treat, and in truth so did I, but I was willing to place my trust in Camilla. She certainly had more experience than I did and I was desperate enough to give anything a try.

Taylor quickly decided that what she wanted most, rather than a day out at a theme park, was a joint makeover, so on Saturday morning, after Emily and Jamie were picked up, we set off together. The beauty salon was only about ten minutes away from our house on foot. Taylor talked all the way there, telling me about school and the children in her class. She really seemed to appreciate having me to herself and I wondered why I hadn't thought of it before.

'I think you'll find she's a bit of a blank canvas,' she chirped to Ranni, the beauty therapist who greeted us at reception, delivering the veiled insult with a mischievous smile and a gentle teasing tone.

I guffawed as I took the seat beside her reclining, cream leather chair. 'And I think you'll find she won't keep quiet enough for you to do what you need to do,' I told the Asian woman standing on the other side of Taylor. Her name tag read Maiya and she was wearing a white coat in the style of a doctor, her hair falling sleek and glossy around the collar. She nodded profusely but smiled blankly, so I wasn't sure whether she understood much English. Taylor grinned, her eyes shining.

Ranni, who had disappeared into a side room, came back out wheeling a trolley. Parking it between our chairs, she draped a long black cape over me, tying it at the neck, and then sat on a stool at my side. She didn't seem to speak English either, but she kept smiling as she filed my nails. I was pleased, in a way, that the beauty therapists weren't chatty types, since it gave Taylor and me the chance to talk.

'It looks as if I've dipped my fingers in some Tippex,' I said, as the beauty therapist painted the tips of my nails white. Taylor giggled, abruptly straightening her face and replacing her smile with a scowl. So fixed in the habit of being disagreeable, I think she found it difficult to let happiness show on her face. When our fingernails were done the therapists moved on to our feet and, unused to having them touched, I found it hard to keep still.

'Have you really never had this done before?' Taylor asked, disbelieving. She told me that, for herself and her mum, it was a regular treat.

'Nope. Why bother? No one sees my feet except me.'

She tried to sneer. I could tell she wanted to, but her eyes were shining and she couldn't really manage it. With no one else to compete with or play up to, it felt as if all the angst between us had been stripped away. Spending time together in a shared activity was relaxing, enjoyable and peculiarly intimate. I was so glad, then, that I had listened to Camilla's advice and made a mental note to thank her for it.

For the next hour, while we were filed, scrubbed and preened, I told her about my own childhood and what it was like being the only girl. She loved it when I lavished her with details of some of the scrapes I got into and was particularly interested to hear about the tricks my brothers played on me. 'My eldest brother, Chris, was the worst practical joker. Or the best, depending on how you look at it.' I gave her a wry smile.

'What then? What did he used to do?'

'Well, once he told me to climb into a box and sit down. I thought he was going to build a camp but then he closed the lip and turned the box upside down. I'm sure that's where my claustrophobia comes from.'

She laughed. 'Cool!'

I wagged my finger at her. 'Don't you go trying that on Reece!'

She widened her eyes. 'As if I would,' she said, smiling sweetly. I chortled and she went on to tell me about one of her family holidays in Wales. 'Nan was there with us, on the beach, and it was so funny, right? 'Cos Dad crept up on me, lifted me up, I was only little but I can still remember it. Then he ran to the water and literally dangled me over the waves. I was screaming and laughing.' She was examining her toes as she spoke, watching as Maiya painted her nails a deep shade of pink. When she glanced at me I could see her eyes shining, cheeks a rosy pink. 'And then, it was so funny yeah, 'cos he slipped over and landed on his backside. He got soaked and Nan creased up!' A shadow fell across her eyes, her smile fading abruptly.

It was the first time she'd ever mentioned her grandmother and Maisie hadn't said anything about extended family members. Usually, when children come into care, social workers try to make sure that links with significant family members are maintained through regular contact. I was about to ask her about it when, as usual, she steered the conversation swiftly in another direction.

Nursing a fragile sense of closeness and keen to avoid spoiling the mood, I let her chatter on without further questions. 'Shall we snuggle up and watch animal programmes when we get home?' she asked, slipping her arm through mine in easy comradeship as we left the salon. I felt a little jot of joy at her use of the plural pronoun; it was something she had never done before. My chest filled with warmth, the feeling tempered quickly afterwards by the suspicion that it wouldn't be too long before my optimism was kicked away.

As soon as we got in she rushed upstairs to fetch her make-up bags, insisting that my face looked naked now that my nails were dressed. Dutifully, I sat on a stool in the living room, pleased that she hadn't even asked to switch the computer on. She kneeled in front of me, painting my skin with powders, creams and liners.

'Ow, careful! You nearly had my eye out.'

'Keep still then!' she snapped, but she was laughing, enjoying herself. When she'd finished she stood up and slipped her forefinger under my chin, tipping my face back. 'Wow, you actually look quite good,' she said, tilting her head in assessment.

'Gee, thanks. Damned by faint praise.'

'What?'

I shook my head and grinned. 'Never mind.'

When she'd finished packing all of her brushes and pencils away she said, 'Now all you need to do is chuck out all your chintzy clothes.'

'Hey,' I said, laughing, and then for some reason I remembered what she had said earlier. 'I know what I meant to ask you. Do you still see your nan? Does she live nearby?'

For a split second I caught a glimpse of bare vulnerability, the pain naked on her face. But then her expression clouded and when she spoke her voice was ragged, her eyes glinting with fury. 'Why do you have to spoil *everything*?' she screamed, her lips pulled back and teeth bared. Spinning on her heel, she stormed from the room and slammed the door behind her.

Chapter Eighteen

It was almost as if little Bailey's screams had travelled miles across town, because just after 3 a.m. two days later, on Sunday morning, I sat upright in bed, muscles shivering in anticipation. Of what, I couldn't say – there was no way I could have known about the disturbing events unfolding seven miles away, but when the telephone rang two hours later, at a little after 5 a.m., it was as if I'd been expecting it. I answered on the second ring.

'Rosie? It's Maisie.'

Disorientated, I frowned, blinking in the still dark room. Had I overslept, I wondered. Social workers rarely called before 9 a.m., unless a foster carer was on the out of hours rota, which I wasn't. 'Erm, yes. Everything OK?'

'No, it's not actually.' There was an unsettling urgency to her voice, surprising, considering the time of day and her usual laid-back drone. She sounded vitally alert as she explained that the police had been called to the Fielding

176

home in the early hours, neighbours concerned about the prolonged, anguished screams coming from their property. 'When officers arrived to conduct a welfare check, they found Mum and Dad in the house and little Bailey alone outside. He'd been zipped up in a tent in the back garden wearing a thin pair of pyjamas and nothing else. The poor little thing was petrified.'

'Oh no,' I said, my chest tightening.

'His parents are under arrest and Bailey's been taken into police protection. So I expect you can guess why I'm calling so early.'

The ball of anger swirling in my chest lowered itself to the pit of my stomach, eased by the prospect of taking practical action and I was certain that being with his brother and sister would go a long way in comforting him. 'Yes, of course. He can come here, no problem.'

'I thought you'd say that, thank you. He's still in a cot so he'll go in with you, if you're OK with that?'

'Absolutely, yes. Poor little mite. Where is he now?'

'We're at the hospital. He's been checked over and the doctors are happy to discharge him. His face is covered in sores but they think it's a result of scratching himself in panic. His fingers are bloody as well, after trying to scrape his way out, but apart from that he's unharmed.' She heaved a sigh and then added 'physically at least'.

As soon as I replaced the receiver I rushed upstairs to the bathroom, washing and dressing as quietly as possible so I didn't wake the children. Fortunately, at 6.30 a.m., when Maisie tapped lightly on the door, they were all still asleep.

'He's exhausted,' she whispered as she climbed the front step into our house, Bailey fast asleep in her arms.

I led the way into the living room, quickly setting a couple of soft cushions at one end of the sofa. Maisie tiptoed across the floor, tongue poking through her lips with the effort of trying not to wake him. We both held our breath as she laid him down, Maisie withdrawing her arm at a snail's pace. As she straightened he stirred and whimpered but I quickly drew a thick fleecy blanket over him, the top brushing his chin. Its soft warmth soothed him back to sleep and he sank further into the sofa, his furrowed brow softening a little.

It was a heartbreaking sight and we stood side by side looking down him for a moment, gripped by a sharp sadness. Hadn't someone once said that every child deserved a parent but not every parent deserved a child? To my mind, at that moment, it seemed a particularly wise observation. My eyes prickled at the sight of the tender skin of his face covered in a series of scratches, some still oozing droplets of blood. Though it had been several hours since he'd been rescued, his eyes were still swollen, those long spiky lashes I remembered from the LAC review barely visible beneath closed lids. His teeth were chattering, even in sleep. Leaning over, I pressed the back of two fingers against the nape of his neck and found that his skin was cool to the touch. Anger soared up to my chest again, its grip so fierce that it actually hurt to think about what he might have witnessed in his short life, what damage might have done to his mind. His bruises and scratches would heal, but how long would it take for the memory of the previous night to fade?

After laying an extra quilt over him and tucking it around his little body to keep the warmth in, I straightened and looked at Maisie. She raised one eyebrow, her lips twisted in a solemn pout. It was one of those times, I think, when words couldn't express the outrage we felt, the disgust, but I could see my own feelings clearly reflected in the social worker's eyes. United in our disbelief, the moment felt to me like a turning point in the relationship between myself and Maisie.

Steam rose from my cup of tea as I sat opposite her in the kitchen, the inevitable can of Red Bull at her side. 'Sorry, Rosie,' she said suddenly, reaching into the deep pocket of her long canvas coat and then tilting the opening towards me to reveal the top of a packet of cigarettes. 'Do you mind if I nip outside?' she asked, glancing at me with an apologetic look.

'Of course not,' I said, opening the back door for her. Although I'd never smoked myself, I almost felt like joining her. She seemed lost in her own thoughts as she paced our small patio and, watching her, my own mind drifted, wondering how anyone could allow any child to suffer, let alone their own flesh and blood. I shuddered when I thought about what must have been going through Bailey's little mind as he shivered alone in the tent. Did he think he'd been deserted for ever? It reminded me about stories I had read of children being bricked up behind the walls of castles and forts in the belief that the sacrifice would make the foundations strong. 'How could they do it to him?' I asked in hushed tones when Maisie came back in. 'Why?'

The social worker shrugged. 'I haven't spoken to the parents personally but according to early reports, Mum's *claiming* that Dad put Bailey in the tent as a punishment to her. Apparently he locked the back door and wouldn't let her out because he suspected she was planning to leave him.'

I sipped at my tea and then cradled the cup against my chest. 'You don't believe her?' Something in Maisie's tone left me feeling she had little sympathy for Claire, the children's mother.

Maisie snorted, suddenly seeming much older. I guessed that was the effect such a challenging job could have on a person. 'I find it helps to keep my expectations low. She'll have her story and he'll have his.'

'But it can't have been her, surely? If their father had wanted to get to Bailey he could have, easily. But there's no way any woman could overpower him.'

Maisie pursed her lips. 'Maybe you're right. But I prefer to assume nothing and question everything. It's just as likely that she's his accomplice, not his victim. Remember what she did to Reece?'

I tilted my head dubiously and she took several large gulps of her drink. She then closed her eyes and released a breath as if it were whisky burning the back of her throat. It was an angry, revealing gesture, one that told me she hadn't yet perfected the art of distancing herself. Her lips were drawn into a tight line, her skin white with fury. She really did care about the children. I felt a sudden urge to give her a hug. 'So what happens now?'

'The Child Abuse Investigation Team have been called in and there'll be an emergency strategy meeting, but there's little doubt that we'll secure an ICO – there's no way any of them can go back home, as things stand.'

If an Interim Care Order was granted by the court, the local authority would share parental responsibility with the Fieldings and gain the right to make decisions with regards to the children. With a whole new set of bureaucratic wheels set in motion, I realised that there would be no quick resolution. My mind flicked to Taylor – how on earth would she feel when she discovered she was stuck with me, at least for the foreseeable future?

Overhead, the floorboards groaned and a loud crash followed. Maisie sucked in a breath and turned sharply on her stool. I darted out of my seat, arriving in the living room as little Bailey sat upright and stared around the room. There was a moment's hesitation when we all seemed to hold our breath and then it came – the piercing, harrowing scream of fear.

Maisie arrived at my side and I took a step backwards, gesturing towards him with my eyes. Since Maisie was the person he had last seen when he fell asleep, I felt he might be less alarmed to see her than me, someone he had only laid eyes on once. With a brief nod, she walked a few steps towards him, just as his screams were turning into hiccoughing sobs. Crouching down so that she was at his eye level and with a fist on the floor for balance, she flattened her other hand, palm upwards and patted the air. 'It's all right, little man. Maisie's here. We went to see the doctor together, do you remember?'

At that moment several pairs of feet thundered down the stairs, and then Taylor, Emily and Reece appeared in the doorway. It was difficult to judge who was more shocked, little Bailey or his older siblings. For several seconds Taylor and Reece stood frozen, their mouths agape. Only Emily was smiling. 'Mum!' she said excitedly, clapping her hands together. 'We've got a new placement!'

'No,' Taylor said quietly, Emily's words breaking through her shock. 'Not a new placement – that's my brother.' She rushed forwards and grabbed him, lifting him into her arms. Sobbing with confused relief, Bailey buried his head into Taylor's shoulder, his little arms tight around her neck. 'There, there,' she crooned like a seasoned mother, rocking gently from one foot to the other. 'It's all right, my love. Ra-ra's here. I'm here.'

Maisie and I exchanged looks. I could see that she was as moved as I was.

The rest of the day passed by in a blur. Not surprisingly, Bailey was overtired. Frequently tearful, his eyes were dim and red-rimmed but he was too distressed to sleep for long. Most of the time he was either in my arms or Taylor's, her care softening the lens I used to view her. It was touching to see how tenderly she handled him and, with the cot and high chair to retrieve from the loft, her help was invaluable.

Torn

I had expected to be fielding questions from her about what had happened, but we were so busy trying to keep Bailey happy that there was barely time to talk between ourselves. The siblings had been told by Maisie that their parents needed a break and I wasn't really sure how much more I could say about what had happened.

It was a relief when 7 o'clock came and as I was getting Bailey into his pyjamas he seemed to feel the same, flopping his wretched and pale face against me without resistance, as if he'd surrendered to the idea of being away from home. 'That's it, sweetie,' I said softly, 'let's get you tucked in now.'

Taylor was at my side as I laid him in the newly erected cot beside my bed, stroking his hair and singing his favourite nursery rhymes. As soon as his little body touched the mattress he rolled onto his side, drew his knees up into the foetal position and slipped his thumb in his mouth, the knuckles of his chubby little fists lacerated and sore. 'Not like that, Rosie,' she said, lifting the blanket I had tucked around him without a trace of her usual asperity. 'He likes it like this,' she said in a soft, sing-song voice, winding the corner of the blanket around his wrist and balling the rest up in the semi-circle between his legs and chest. 'You like to hug your blankie, don't you, Bailey?' She pulled his quilt up over his chin.

'Ah, that looks lovely and snugly. Night, night, sweetheart,' I said in a hushed tone. As soon as we turned to leave though, he sat up and burst into tears, Taylor's carefully positioned quilt and blanket falling into disarray.

'I'll stay with him,' Taylor whispered, sitting on the floor beside the cot and reaching through the bars to hold his hand. 'It's what I do at home,' she said, and Bailey seemed to know the drill. In an instant he had stopped crying and laid himself down, doing his best to rearrange his covers with the help of his sister's restricted hand.

Chapter Nineteen

By Monday morning, the novelty of seeing a new side to Taylor was beginning to wear off. Having lost patience with my vague explanations, her questions about the events of the previous day were becoming increasingly probing. 'But you must know something-er,' she insisted as I tried to get her wriggly brother dressed. 'The social wouldn't just dump another kid on you without telling you why. I'm not stupid, Rosie, and if you don't tell me what's happened I'm gonna bunk school and go find out for myself.'

Having loosened my grip on Bailey, he arched his back and slid from my lap. I smiled, despite the lateness of the hour. A big bundle of warmth and cuddles, I loved having him around. He was gaining confidence in his new surroundings, although he had barely eaten anything since he'd arrived. The only food he accepted with any enthusiasm was yoghurt, but at least he had drunk plenty of milk. I watched him delve into a basket of toys I'd rescued from the loft and then looked up at his sister. She was bound to be concerned, I understood that, and it did seem unfair to fob her off with weak explanations, but it was difficult to know what else to tell her. All I had done was repeat what Maisie had told them when Bailey first arrived – that her parents weren't in a position to care for him and contact would be arranged as soon as possible.

Telling her the truth about what had happened wasn't going to help her feel any better, I knew that much. When it came to children, honesty wasn't always the best policy, although Taylor had a right to know something. I needed to talk to Maisie and come up with an explanation, if not the whole truth then at least a watered down version of it. 'I know you're worried, honey and I understand.' I bit my lip and stood up, walking over to the fireplace. Bailey crawled between and around my legs like a cat as I reached into the box where Taylor's phone was kept. 'Tell you what. You can take your phone to school today.' I was holding it aloft and she made a grab for it. I pulled it away, holding it out to the side. She grinned and rolled her eyes. 'Uh-oh, just as a one-off, mind,' I said, offering it to her. She snatched it from my hand, thanking me hurriedly when I gave her a stern look. 'I'll call Maisie first thing this morning and see what I can find out and then I'll text you, OK? So if you switch your phone on at break time you should find a message from me.'

She held it flat in her palm, staring at it with reverence as if it were a winning lottery ticket, then slipped it into her school rucksack.

It was just after two o'clock when I finally managed to get hold of Maisie. Knowing that Taylor would probably be on tenterhooks until she heard some news I had sent her a couple of texts, one just before break time and then one around midday, telling her that I would keep trying to get some information for her. She sent me a little upside-down smiley face in response, the X after it showing me how grateful she was to hear something. As it happened, it looked as if we wouldn't have to tell them anything ourselves – Maisie had arranged an after-school contact session. 'They'll be collected straight from school and taken to the contact centre. Dad's still in custody so it's just with Mum.'

Maisie went on to explain that she had spent the whole morning with Claire, who had finally opened up about her relationship, admitting what she'd always denied – that her husband was a violent bully. 'I can't believe what those kids have been through, Rosie,' Maisie said, but I could tell from her tone that her sympathies didn't lie with either Mum or Dad. 'She reckons he was responsible for Taylor's injuries. Apparently she was trying to defend her mum and got caught in the crossfire.'

My heart lurched. It was as I'd suspected, but to hear that it happened because Taylor was trying to defend her mum, well, that made it even sadder.

'We've secured an ICO through the court. Claire's gone into a refuge and I've organised a meeting with her the day after tomorrow. I'd like you to attend if you can. Mum's concerned about some things Taylor's been telling her and I think you'd best hear it for yourself.'

* * *

Without the extra school run to fit in I got home early with Emily and Jamie that afternoon. We went straight into the garden, Jamie making the most of my undivided attention and telling me about a practical joke some of the boys in the year above had carried out on his teacher. With only two children to fill me in on their day, and Bailey, who, for a toddler, watched too much and smiled too little, it seemed eerily quiet. Once or twice I felt a little jolt of discomfort, my subconscious warning me that I may have forgotten something vital. Leaning forwards, my eyes darted quickly to and fro as I tried to work out what it was and then I remembered that Taylor and Reece were at contact. It was peaceful though, hearing Emily and Jamie's relaxed banter, punctuated here and there with Bailey's cute little noises. Sitting in my favourite wicker chair and listening to it all, I felt more relaxed than I had in weeks.

Enter Taylor Fielding.

It started with an assault on the door bell, her finger still grinding it to a pulp even after I had opened the door. The ferocious scowl on her face as she barged past me and ran up the stairs told me that the meeting with their mother hadn't gone well, but by the time I turned back to ask the contact supervisor about it, a short, nervous woman with a harassed frown, she had disappeared from view.

Reece slipped in quietly, looking up at me with mournful eyes as I closed the front door. I held my arms open and he buried his head into my chest, letting out a sad little puff of air. When I pulled away and cupped my hands around his face all he said was, 'My chest feels too big.' I had noticed it was something he said when things got rough – emotion swelling up inside him so that his chest literally ached with sadness. They hadn't seen their mother for well over two weeks, so I had expected some sort of reaction. Children often adjusted quickly to their new environment when they came into foster care, but contact was a disruption of their routine, reminding them of the problems at home and the struggles that their own parents were going through.

Contact had taken place in the community, as sometimes happens, with a contact supervisor following the family around while they spent time together. According to Reece, they ate their tea in a fast-food restaurant, which seemed ironic, considering one of Mum's complaints against me. It was also unfortunate – since Taylor had eaten, there was no reason to insist that she came down to join us for dinner.

After giving Bailey his bath and putting him to bed, I went up to check on her, hopeful that the hour's solitude in her room might have helped to calm her. 'Leave me alone!' she screamed, when I tapped on her door and opened it a crack.

Almost three weeks in her company had taught me that the wisest thing to do, whenever she kicked off, was to walk away and let her calm down. When Reece went to bed I tapped softly on her door, left some water on the floor just outside and asked her to get ready for bed. The resultant grunt assured me that she was fine, and so I let her be.

Halfway through the ten o'clock news that evening though, just as I was beginning to nod off on the sofa, there was a loud thumping noise on the stairs. I started and looked up, surprised to see Taylor standing at the threshold of the living room. Blinking, I quickly sat up. 'Taylor, is everything –'

But I didn't finish the sentence because she wheeled across the carpet, threw herself onto the sofa about two feet away from me and clamped her head in her hands. I grabbed the TV remote, turned the volume down and then turned back to her. 'What is it, Taylor?'

Slowly she let her hands fall to her lap, her mouth working with the effort of keeping her emotions in check. It was tempting to take her into my arms and soothe her but I stopped myself, wary of repulsing her or frightening her off. To some children, a hug was not a comfort but a prelude to something sinister and, without knowing Taylor's past, I wasn't going to make assumptions. 'I can see you're upset, sweetie,' I said gently. 'Naming the feeling' was a technique mentioned in one of the child psychology books I had read when registering as a foster carer.

The idea was to replace the automatic response people tended to give an upset child – 'Aw, never mind, it's OK' or 'There, there, it's all right, don't be sad' – with a few words that demonstrated that their feelings were valid and understandable. By labelling the emotion, the child would then perhaps be more able to recognise their own feelings and therefore find a mechanism for regulating them. 'Whatever it is, you can tell me.' I rolled my bottom lip under my top teeth. 'I'd like to help,' I added, forcing myself to use words instead of actions.

Torn

She swallowed down a sob and held her breath so long that her eyes began to bulge. My heart flew out to her.

'Let it out, honey.' I reached out a hand and rested it a fraction of an inch from her leg. My fingers flexed out to pat her; I couldn't help myself.

All of a sudden the dam burst. After a long, loud exhalation the sobs came, so violent that her shoulders trembled. Tears rolled down both cheeks and she sagged, laying her head against a cushion on my lap. She cried until her voice grew hoarse, until the cushion below her face became wet. I stroked her hair and whispered words of comfort, though I can't remember what they were. Eventually she sat up, her hair darkened with tears. She began to pant like a woman in labour, trying to prevent further sobs. When her breathing finally slowed she looked at me, sucked in some more air and then managed to splutter, 'Mum's gone into a refuge and they don't take dogs so she's given Jimmy away!'

'Oh no, I'm so sorry, love.' I reached out for her and she threw herself into my arms, sobbing on my shoulder. When Maisie told me about Claire going into a refuge, I hadn't even thought about what might happen to the family's dog. Moving into a refuge was a courageous, positive step for her mother to take, but it meant yet another loss for the children to bear. Not for the first time I felt a surge of pity for Taylor, her brother and all the children moved around like pawns on a chessboard, because the people around them couldn't (or wouldn't) stop creating mayhem. 'That's tough on you. I know how much you loved him.'

She pulled back and looked at me, her face a mass of blotches. 'I did!' she wailed, gulping down huge sobs. 'I loved him *so* much, Rosie. I hate my mum! I hate her! Why did she have to wind Dad up all the time? None of this would of happened if she'd just kept quiet like she used to.'

'Wind him up? How?'

She threw up her hands. 'I dunno do I? She used to keep quiet and he'd only go mad when Chelsea lost but lately she's been fighting back. She just made everything worse.'

It occurred to me then that she hadn't ever had the slightest interest in football – all the while, when she'd been desperate to find out the score of Saturday matches, she'd been desperately fearful for her mum if they lost. Suddenly, I felt overwhelmingly sad. I smoothed her tears away with the pad of my thumb and then enfolded her hands in my own, holding them tightly in my lap. 'I understand you're angry, honey. And I know it hurts, but your mum has been very brave. I know it's difficult to appreciate that when you're hurting inside but she's done something that many women never manage to do.'

She stared at me for a moment and then her face crumpled in another sob. 'Oh, Rosie. I was so horrible to Mum at contact. All she's ever done is be kind to me and I told her she made me sick. I didn't even say goodbye, even though she was crying. I'm so horrible! Literally everyone hates me. Why am I so disgusting?'

Her words rang with familiarity, and then I remembered why I recognised them – she was repeating exactly what had been said to her on Myspace. It was the first time I truly appreciated the power that a line of black letters across a screen could inflict, magnifying her own insecurities and immortalising the abuse for future friends, lovers and employers to pick over and dissect. I felt a flicker of undirected anger towards the faceless strangers online, too cowardly to even use their real names. And then I felt a flash of irritation towards Taylor. Why did she continue to use the site, when those messages were clearly seeping in, slowly eroding her childhood away? And why was she corresponding with people she didn't even appear to know? I had heard from other parents that children had a tendency to accept friend requests from strangers on their social-media accounts, to present a picture of popularity, but I found it all a little baffling. She needed to stop questioning her own self-worth and start doubting her so-called friends. But then again, why did anyone stay in an abusive relationship? It was natural for a child of her age to want to feel a part of it all and to fit in with her peers.

Since fostering I had noticed that childhood seemed to be getting shorter, at least for many of the children I looked after. It struck me as ironic that Dickens and other campaigners had worked so hard to construct a childhood for children, and yet almost two centuries on it was fading away again.

'No, Taylor, you're not any of those things,' I said firmly, hoping to leave no room in her head for doubt. I wanted to tell her that she shouldn't measure her own worthiness using the opinions of others, but without admitting to invading her privacy it was difficult to be that direct. I wanted her to understand that her own happiness should be independent from her online 'friends'. I thought that if I could teach her to value what was on the inside, she might just grow up expecting others to show her the same courtesy.

But what chance did I or anyone have of convincing her that beauty was transient, when she was being distantly programmed by the magazines and glamour books she was addicted to. 'You're an intelligent, loving girl with a wonderful sense of fun. You're fiercely protective of your little brothers and loyal to your family. You've just had a rough time of it lately, that's all. No one can be lovely all of the time.'

'You really think so? How can you tell? I'm horrible to you.'

'Hmm, you do keep it well hidden,' I said, smiling with a raised brow. 'I'll grant you that.'

She giggled and sobbed all at the same time, the sounds colliding in her throat. After fetching the duvet from her bed, we sat side by side on the sofa for another hour or so, watching animal programmes that I had recorded. On screen an officer from the RSPCA was talking to an unseen interviewer and simultaneously rescuing a kitten trapped inside a thin sewerage pipe. The officer, a bearded, paunchy man in his fifties, sounded choked as he tried to couch his outrage in a gentle tone so as not to alarm the frightened pet. From the corner of my eye I could see fresh tears streaming down Taylor's face. All I could think, as my heart squeezed with pity was, what on earth had happened? Why was Claire suddenly fighting back?

Chapter Twenty

'I'll have him,' my mother said the next morning when I told her about Taylor's dog. 'Find out where he was taken and I'll go and get him.'

'You can't do that, Mum!' I exclaimed, even though it was an idea that had occurred to me. I'd immediately dismissed it through fear of exacerbating Jamie's asthma symptoms, but the desire had been there and I knew that Mum, like most people, hated the idea of children suffering as much as I did.

We were talking on the phone and I could tell from the splashing and clinking noises that Mum was washing up, probably with the phone cradled between her shoulder and ear. As we spoke, Bailey toddled over and wrapped his arms around my leg. Switching the handset to loudspeaker, I set it down on the worktop in the kitchen and broke a biscuit in half for Bailey.

'Ku-ku,' he said by way of thanks, pushing the semi-circle into his mouth with the flat of his hand.

'Careful. Not too much, Bailey,' I warned, relieved that he had added biscuits to his list of things he was willing to eat. It might not have been the most nutritious of foods, but at least it was something solid. 'Sorry, Mum. You're still not fully recovered yourself yet and –'

'Oh, don't be daft,' she interrupted, but when we went on to discuss it seriously, it occurred to us that when the placement eventually ended, depending on where Taylor and Reece moved onto, they were likely to go through the heartbreak of separation all over again. Deciding it would probably only prolong the agony, we decided against it, but I thanked her for the offer, and then we made arrangements for her to look after Bailey while I attended the meeting with Claire and Maisie the following day. Excited to meet the toddler, she readily agreed.

Taylor hadn't been far from my thoughts all morning after I dropped her at school. It was hard to forget her look of distress on her face as she told me about losing Jimmy. Nor had I forgotten her desperation to make amends with her mother. Despite her own pain, she possessed the capacity to feel concern for other people, something I found immensely reassuring.

Before going to bed she had sent her mum a text saying she was sorry and Claire had replied immediately, her message sweet and loving. It played on my mind, the inconsistencies in the relationship they shared. From a distance Claire seemed loving and attentive, and seemed to have a close bond with her children, yet she had attacked Reece so ferociously that the bruises still hadn't quite faded.

Torn

Around 2 p.m., after Bailey had woken from his nap, I strapped him into his car seat and drove to the local authority civic centre to collect a spare key to the Fielding family home. After finding out that she would be staying with me longer than expected, Taylor had asked whether she could go and collect some more of her things. Maisie felt that it would be too unsettling for her to return home, however briefly, so I had agreed to go while the children were at school.

The streets grew wider as I drove further away from the town centre, the sky darkening with the promise of rain. Every time I glanced in the rear-view mirror Bailey rewarded me with a wide smile, his big blue eyes lighting up his whole angelic, pudgy face. They were coming more easily now, his smiles, and I was reminded of something I'd read about blind babies and their smiles, which begin to appear around four weeks old. I liked that thought, that a baby might smile because happiness was bubbling up from within – it wasn't simply a case of copying those around them.

By the time I pulled up outside number 14, a wide terraced house with wooden slated blinds at each of the windows, the skies had opened. Rain fell softly onto Bailey as I lifted him out of his seat, beading his honey-brown hair.

I stood for a moment at the gate, looking up at the house with my stomach swirling. Blinking against the misty rain, I tried to work out why I was feeling so anxious. Something didn't feel quite right to me, almost as if I expected to walk in and hear the sounds of young, pleading voices, or the thump of a hard fist meeting soft flesh.

Bailey protested at my hesitation and wriggled from my arms, running towards the door that was so familiar to him but strange to me. As I followed, I thought I saw a light flickering behind one of the blinds. A shadow moved across the path at my feet and I stopped, my breath catching in my throat.

Forcing a slow breath to steady myself, I jogged after Bailey, sidestepping an overturned scooter that was sticking out from one of the neatly pruned bushes lining the path. It was a good thing I had a dissenting toddler as my companion; he was the perfect distraction from the anxiety running through me.

As I walked into the hallway I realised what had been nagging me as I looked up at the neat, well-presented house – it was my own prejudices. I had been expecting squalor, or at least somewhere slightly unkempt with a windswept garden and an air of disarray – highly unfairly, as it turned out. In the hallway, where I expected empty cans of fizzy drinks and cigarette packets to be strewn, a mahogany side table and large urn filled with dried flowers stood. In the living room, instead of overflowing ashtrays and mouse droppings, there was a nest of coffee tables and a solid, boxy leather sofa, flanked on both sides with enormous bright orange beanbags. On the floor in the middle of the room there was a large animal print rug and the cushions on two armchairs were striped black and white, both fluffy. I had to admit, the place was spotless. There wasn't a single sign that the owners had left in a hurry – until I turned and peered through the recently polished wooden blinds hanging across French windows at one end of the room. A neat, well-maintained garden was visible through the slats and, chillingly, the zip-up entrance to a small tent was open, a small slipper abandoned halfway between the canvas door and the house.

Worried that the sight might remind Bailey of his recent trauma, I spun around and reached for him, carrying him up the stairs. Halfway up, I stopped, a photo fixed to the wall of the Fielding family drawing my attention. In the picture, a much younger Taylor was standing in front of Nick and Claire, one of their hands resting on each of her shoulders. As I studied her face, trying to see if I could spot signs of sadness behind her smile, I became aware that my pulse was rising. The realisation slowly filtered upwards, from my churning stomach to my brain – I knew exactly where I'd seen Nick Fielding before.

'Up! Up!' Bailey shouted, interrupting my thoughts.

'OK, up we go,' I said, my gaze lingering on the photo as my feet moved up the stairs.

There were four doors dotted along the hallway, each slightly ajar. The first was a small but gleaming bathroom, not a rubber duck or stack of cups in sight. The master bedroom next to it was spacious and uncluttered; the only sign of the presence of children a wooden cot against one wall, with silver and burgundy wallpaper behind. 'Mama,' said Bailey with a little whimper. I cupped a hand on the warm nape of his neck and planted a kiss on his forehead, my heart giving a little squeeze.

It was as I turned to leave the room that I spotted the dark-red spatter pattern across the wall above the double bed. My eyes followed the line to a stain on the cream carpet beside a bedside table, the centre darker than the outer ripples. My stomach flipped at the sight and I pictured their mother on her knees, trying her best to erase the tell-tale signs of secret abuse. I suddenly remembered what Taylor had said about her mother fighting back. Walking steadily along the hall to the children's bedroom with Bailey balanced on my hip, my mind puzzled over it again – what had spurred a habitually submissive woman into sudden retaliation?

Feeling a tiny pulse of shame (mild enough to ignore) I sat Bailey in his highchair with a snack when we got in from the school run, carrying him in it from the kitchen to the computer desk. He screeched with excited delight, making clip-clop noises with his tongue. I had encouraged the others to play in the garden under the pretext of giving me some space to prepare dinner, but the casserole I'd put in the oven needed no attention.

A quick Google search confirmed what I'd realised earlier – Nick Fielding was a convicted burglar. It transpired that I had recognised him from mug shots I had seen while working for the police. He had been imprisoned about fifteen years earlier and when I clicked on another link I was taken to a local newspaper site reporting on several convictions for drugs offences. As I read on, something Taylor had said came back to me – 'My dad buys me anything I want.' Some of the mysteries of Taylor's past were beginning to fall into place.

It was as I settled Bailey into his cot (after a whole bowl of chicken casserole and two triangles of bread for supper – hurray!) that I realised how quiet Reece had been since we got home from school. While Taylor had been delighted to get more of her things from home, he had seemed disinterested, leaving most of the toys untouched in the corner of the living room. Now, sitting on the edge of his bed and pulling his pyjamas on, I noticed that his skin was paler than usual. I felt his forehead with the back of my hand. 'Oh, you're hot, sweetie. Do you feel OK?'

'Yep,' he said, climbing into bed. But his pupils were as tiny as pinpricks and there was a slight greenish tinge to the delicate skin beneath his eyes. 'Can we play that game you were telling me about, Rosie, instead of reading a story?'

'Of course we can, if you're feeling up to it.' Taylor had reacted noisily to the break-up of her parents and the loss of their dog, but Reece had barely blinked. The child psychology books I had read a couple of years earlier had armed me with an inventive supply of games, a mental box of tricks that could be tailored to help reluctant talkers open up. A few minutes later I was sitting on the end of Reece's bed with a box of farm animals and equipment between us. 'This game is called the Field of Dreams,' I said, picking out some loose pieces of fencing.

'OK,' he said, rising to his haunches. His drooping eyelids perked up a little.

'We have to fence three fields off for the farmer, so that he has somewhere to put his horses.'

'Right,' Reece said, his forehead corrugated in concentration. He rummaged around in the box, pulling out fences and horses.

'Great,' I said, 'so here we have the Feel Good Field,' pointing to the field beside his left leg. 'In the middle is the Field of Worries and at the end is the Field of Dreams. What we need to do now is give each of our horses a home.'

'Wow, that's easy,' he said, ready to drop his handful of horses into the nearest field.

'Ah, but it's not that simple! First, you have to choose which field you're going to put the horse into. And then, as you put one into, say, the Feel Good Field, you need to think of something that makes you happy. If he's going into the Field of Worries –'

He shot his hand into the air, as if he were still at school. 'I know, I know! I need to think of something that makes me worry!'

'Exactly! So, shall we get started?'

He nodded vigorously, dropping four horses instantly into the Feel Good Field. 'The little foal is Bailey,' he said. 'And the big horses are Taylor, Emily and Jamie.'

'Ah, that's nice,' I said, smiling.

He stared at the horses in front of him for a while, tilting his head from one side to the other as he carefully selected them. 'I'm going to put this brown one in the Field of

Worries,' he said, 'because he has the same colour hair as me and I worry a *lot*.'

I laughed, cupping my hand at the back of his head. 'You are a bit of a worry bunny aren't you?'

He nodded earnestly, his forehead rumpling in a slight frown. He was taking it all very seriously, bless him. 'I don't like it when Mummy and Daddy fight,' he said after a moment, laying one horse carefully in the Field of Worries. I had thought that Reece might need coaxing to get him talking and I had planned to conceal some probing questions in a litany of gentle ones. But it seemed that there was no need for subterfuge with him. Grabbing a few more animals, he put them in one by one. 'I'm worried about Jimmy. It's hard, being sent away, even if your new owner is nice.' He threw me a smile then and leaned forward, brushing his head onto my leg. When he sat up his expression was grave. 'What if he thinks we don't love him anymore?'

'I'm sure he doesn't think that, honey. You're staying with me at the moment but Mummy and Daddy know that you still love them.'

He pouted, considering that for a moment. 'Taylor doesn't love Daddy. He looks at her funny.'

My chest constricted. 'Funny? In what way?'

He tilted his head and shrugged. 'Er, dunno, but it makes my tummy go funny.' Picking up another horse, he kissed it and laid it in the field. There was barely any room left in the Field of Worries and so he piled them one on top of the other. 'And I don't like it when Mummy hurts us.'

I nodded, giving him a sad but, I hoped, encouraging smile. 'So, what would you most like to happen? How could we get the horses from here,' I said, pointing to the Field of Worries, 'into one of the other fields? The Field of Dreams is for horses with ideas of how we could help to make things better for you.'

He threw his bottom lip out and strummed it with his fingers. 'Erm, I wish that Daddy would like Taylor again, like he used to. I wish that Mummy and Daddy would stop fighting and I wish we could get Jimmy back.' It was funny, the way young children interpreted domestic violence. Even though one parent was much stronger than the other, it always seemed to be 'Mummy and Daddy fighting' as if the battle was even.

My heart squeezed again. A moment's peace didn't seem like too much for a little boy to ask.

By the time we'd packed the animals and fencing away he looked exhausted. There were the usual questions of course, as I tucked him in. 'Rosie, did you know that people used to clean their teeth with twigs and horsehair?' and 'People say they're going to hit the hay when they're going to bed because they used to sleep on old sacks stuffed with it.' But his usual enthusiasm for facts was absent, his tone dim.

After giving him some Calpol and a hug I switched the light off. 'Night, night, honey.'

'Rosie?' he called out before I'd reached the stairs.

'Yes?' I called out in a loud whisper. 'Bailey's asleep so don't yell.'

Torn

'Did you know that people say "Night, night, sleep tight" because mattresses used to be held up with rope and it used to come loose when they rolled over?'

'Really?' I said, giving him the surprised tone he was after. 'How interesting! Now, go to sleep.'

But two hours later he was awake and crying with a sore throat, blocked-up nose and headache. 'I want Mummy,' he croaked, tears rolling down his flushed cheeks. 'Mummy always tells me stories when I'm ill and makes me all betterer.'

'Don't worry sweetie,' I said, stroking his hair back from his forehead. His cropped style was growing out and falling softly over his ears. 'I'll look after you.'

When I trudged back up the stairs a few minutes later armed with ibuprofen, Taylor was in the room, stroking his head and checking his symptoms. Never slow to lash out at her younger brother with harsh words (and the odd kick, when my back was turned), it always surprised me how quickly she switched to a maternal role, if ever he was genuinely upset or ill. 'Has he had Calpol?' she demanded. 'He always has Calpol when he's got a temperature.'

'Yes, Taylor,' I answered patiently. 'But he can't have any more of that for now.'

She nodded curtly, keeping a stern eye on me as I administered the ibuprofen.

'It's not working,' Reece howled after swallowing the clear liquid. 'My throat still really hurts.' Throwing the covers back and rising to his knees, his eyes fixed on mine, pleading for help. 'I can't breathe!' he shrieked, waving his arms in front of his face in panic. 'My throat is blocked.'

Taylor's eyes widened, catching his hysteria. 'Do something, Rosie! He can't breathe! He can't breathe!!'

'Hey! Stop panicking! You are breathing, honey, or you wouldn't be able to talk. Now, would you like me to have a word with some special people who are experts at dealing with worried, poorly children?'

Reece paused, his arms coming to rest at his sides. He frowned, slumped down a little so that his bottom came to a rest on the back of his calves. 'What people?' He gasped. Taylor raised her eyebrows in an arch.

'Ah, well, let's settle you against here,' I said with an air of mystery, arranging his pillows in an upside down V. 'And I'll go and have a word with them. They're tiny, so it takes a while to find them, but if I ask nicely they might give me some of their special medicine. It always works brilliantly.'

'Where are they?' he asked, watching me carefully. He wasn't sure whether to believe me, but I noticed that his breathing had slowed. Suggestibility was one of the most endearing, delightful traits in young children and I couldn't help but smile as I left the room and called out, 'At the bottom of the garden.' I ran downstairs to look for a menthol rub, convinced that Taylor was telling him that I was talking rubbish. But as I came back up the stairs I heard her elaborating on my tale, telling him that the little people were experts at finding the right flowers with magical properties for helping children. My heart swelled with affection for her, touched that she was generous enough to allow her brother to continue believing in fairies, even though I suspected she had long since given up believing in anything magical herself.

Back in his room, Reece was much calmer and intrigued when I rubbed the cream onto the soles of his feet. 'Why are you doing that?' he asked with a croaky laugh.

'It works best this way apparently. I'm just doing what I'm told.'

When both feet were coated I tucked him back under the duvet and sat beside him. Taylor lay beside him on his other side. 'I think it's working already, Rosie. It must be magic!' Reece exclaimed.

'It always works,' I said, smiling and patting his arm.

He was asleep within minutes, mouth open, breathing raspy but even. 'Come on then,' I whispered to Taylor as I rose to my feet. 'Let's get back to bed.'

'Er, Rosie,' she said quietly, 'I think you'd better take this away.' She pointed to the menthol cream I had left on Reece's bedside cabinet. 'It says Tesco on the lid.'

I giggled. 'Oh goodness, you're right!' I whispered under my breath. She looked at me and smiled, her expression filled with unexpected warmth and affection. My spirit danced a little jig and I put my arm around her shoulder as we walked along the hall, side by side. Both united in our concern for her little brother, I was transformed into her temporary ally. Words could hardly express how good that felt.

Chapter Twenty-One

Reece was still poorly the following morning. Hot to the touch, he lay on the sofa with half-closed eyes, looking very sorry for himself. Fortunately, my mum had the morning free, so she came over to sit with the patient and take care of Bailey while I did the school run and went on to my meeting with Claire. At the sound of the doorbell, Taylor grabbed Bailey and ran into the hall, eager to introduce him. She revelled in my mum's delighted reaction, asking him to perform various 'tricks' like a proud parent.

After dropping Emily and Jamie off, however, she withdrew into herself, answering sullenly when I made a jokey reference to our fairy story of the previous night. As usual, she left the car without a backward glance after I wished her a good day, entering the playground with her head bowed low. I watched her disappear into a group of chattering children, part of me aching at the sight of such an unhappy child. There were errant thoughts too, like was it really too much to ask for her to say goodbye, or at least turn and nod in acknowledgement?

It was her unpredictable coldness that got to me, repeatedly throwing me off-balance – strange really, because on the surface Taylor and I got on well. In terms of humour we were on the same wavelength, laughing throughout the day at things that no one else found particularly funny, but our rapport was transient, never translating into anything solid.

My mind gnawed away at it as I drove towards town and, keen to avoid fretting over the uncomfortable meeting that awaited me, I was only too happy to let it. Maisie had arranged for us to meet in a discreet back-street cafe several miles from the children's school and, crucially, the Fielding family home. As far as I knew, Nick Fielding was still in custody, but I guessed that Maisie felt there was no point in taking any chances. Wanting a short walk to gather myself, I parked the car down a lane about a quarter of a mile from our meeting place. It began to drizzle as I passed a small play park, the sky a monotonous grey. I carried on past a series of unremarkable streets, stopping at the end of a small side road where residential and commercial buildings stood side by side.

A group of teenagers, who had been passing a cigarette between themselves, started kicking a tin can from one to the other. As they parted, I spotted a small woman, roughly my own height, walking in my direction from the opposite end of the street. Immediately convinced that it was Claire, my heart went out to her at first glance. Too far away for me to analyse her expression, it was the way she walked that got to me – head dipped and shoulders slumped. She looked totally defeated, as if it was an effort to put one foot in front of the other. Unhappy, grey and downtrodden, I suddenly worried that I might not find the right words to say to her.

As she drew near she lifted her head, slowing her step when she spotted me. We came to a halt a few feet away from each other, on the opposite side of the road to the cafe. 'Claire?' I said, smiling and holding out my hand. I knew it was her by then; Taylor was the image of her. 'I'm Rosie.' Across the street, a flock of birds took flight. Claire gasped and spun around, her hand flying to her chest. When she turned back she laughed shakily and touched her hand lightly on my own in the lightest of shakes. She was wearing black silk gloves, despite the mild day.

'Hello, Rosie,' she said, her tone unsteady but not, I was relieved to find, unfriendly. She still looked startled.

We crossed the road in silence, an imprint of her well-tailored grey trousers and smart black jacket lingering in my vision as we made our way over to the cafe. Her face was as I'd imagined it: an older version of Taylor's in many ways, only a little softer, with her light-coloured hair falling in soft waves to her shoulders, instead of scraped back into a harsh ponytail like her daughter. In every other way though, she was exactly the opposite of what I'd expected. I'm not sure what that was exactly, since I knew that domestic violence was no respecter of money or class, but her sophisticated clothes and reserved stance didn't seem to fit the template of 'abused wife' in my mind.

Torn

Up close, the cafe had an uncared for feel to it. From the cracked glass in the door to the battered greying window frames, the building looked more like a squat than commercial premises. Claire looked out of place in the grimy surroundings, as if a cabbie had made a mistake and dropped her off on the wrong side of town. She patted her hair nervously as I opened the door and held it back for her, and then stood in the middle of the cafe looking lost. I was glad to see that the interior, in stark contrast to the outside, was bright and cheerful, with several tall potted plants dotted around the place. Cinnamon and coffee scented the air, and the tables, all covered with bright vinyl cloths, were spotless.

Since one of the purposes of the meeting was to run through the list of grievances Claire had about my standards of care, I was glad that Maisie had already arrived – it was the sort of meeting that would be uncomfortable without a mediator present. Sitting at a table nestled in the corner of the cafe, I guessed she had chosen the spot because it was far enough from the counter to allow us to talk without being overheard. The social worker lifted her hand in greeting when she saw me, nodding grimly when she caught sight of Claire. The only other customer, an elderly lady with a china cup and small silver teapot on the table in front of her, took no notice as Claire and I crossed the linoleum floor towards the table.

Maisie half stood when we reached her, tilting her head towards the other empty chairs. Deliberately, I took a seat on the opposite side of the table to Maisie, so that Claire wouldn't have to sit facing both of us, something I felt might be intimidating. Maisie and I made small talk after a waitress took our order, mainly about what the children had been up to over the holidays.

Claire took the chair next to mine, sitting gingerly, as if her bones were sore. She kept her coat on and head bent over. She even kept her gloves on, as if she'd rather be ready to bolt at any moment. Even so, I turned towards her as I spoke, trying to include her – it was *her* children we were talking about, after all. 'Bailey's not been eating that well though,' I said, after telling her how nice it was to see how much Taylor and Reece enjoyed their food. 'I was hoping you could give me a few tips.' With previous placements I had found that asking parents for advice seemed to please them more than anything else, helping them to feel that, at least in some way, they were still involved in their children's lives.

Claire seemed taken aback to be consulted. She stared at me for a moment and then glanced at Maisie. 'He is a bit of a fussy eater,' she said slowly. 'He tends to prefer his food finely mashed.'

Maisie scowled, probably concerned that a child of Bailey's age was still eating pureed foods, but she was distracted by the waitress who had arrived with our hot drinks. When the young woman disappeared into the kitchen I carried on chatting about the children and Claire seemed to relax after a few minutes, laughing out loud when I told her about the banter between Taylor and the rest of us. 'That's just typical of her,' she chuckled, removing her sunglasses and wiping under her eyes with her index finger. 'She's got an answer for everything.'

My own smile vanished immediately. One of her eyes was swollen and red, the other half closed in a blue and purple misshapen slit. It looked as if a child had ransacked a make-up bag and attacked her with loaded brushes while she was asleep. Without her glasses on I noticed how thin her skin was, stretched tight across her cheekbones. Even the whites of her eyes were pink. It was horrifying to see and I looked quickly away, embarrassment and anger reddening my cheeks.

The atmosphere changed, becoming heavy with solemnity. Maisie, her jaw hardening, flipped open the bulky A4 pad in front of her and slid a biro out from her wiry hair. She was wearing a light-coloured, crocheted cardigan over a floral blouse but she looked anything but soft as she ran her eyes over Claire. 'So, how do you want to do this?' she asked, not a trace of tenderness in her voice. 'Shall we run through your concerns first, and then move on to the new contact arrangements?' She turned several pages of the pad over and pulled out a sheaf of loose papers with small typescript on.

Claire's eyes flicked towards the door as if mentally planning an escape route and I felt another flash of sympathy for her – I often felt uncomfortable in meetings, particularly as those arranged by social services tended to be highly charged with emotion. Besides, criticising a complete stranger was difficult enough for anyone, let alone for someone who had recently emerged from the shadow of domestic abuse and was probably at that moment pretty close to rock bottom. Claire shifted in her seat and stared at the papers upside down on the table in front of her.

Maisie glared at her without a glimmer of sympathy and Claire's mouth began to twitch. Suddenly she burst into tears. I looked at Maisie in surprise and then held out my hand to Claire, hesitating when I caught the social worker's look of disapproval. I went ahead and patted her shoulder anyway.

'I'm sorry,' she sniffed, looking sideways at me.

I looked at Maisie. It was clear she wasn't going to say anything comforting so I handed Claire a napkin, groping for something to say. 'It's OK,' I said eventually.

'Oh, Christ, I'm such a mess. What must you think of me?'

Maisie gave her a non-committal look then pressed her lips together. I glanced between them, feeling I had to say something. 'I know things have been difficult,' I ventured.

She turned to me, dabbing her eyes with the tissue. 'They have. They really have. I'm sorry about all that,' she said, waving at the papers with her empty hand. 'But when Taylor told us she was unhappy, what else could we do? I didn't want to complain but Nick –' She stopped, her expression anguished.

'When it comes to children, you can't do right for doing wrong.' I don't know why I said that. I wasn't sure I even understood what it meant, but it sounded appropriate and Claire seemed to appreciate it.

'Exactly!' She was nodding vigorously, almost excitedly, as if at last, someone understood her. 'But I know you're probably doing your best. Taylor can be a bit' – she licked her lips – 'difficult.'

'As I said the other day, Claire,' Maisie chipped in, 'it's not unusual for children to complain about where they're placed.' The skin beside the social worker's right eye was pierced with a small silver ring. She fiddled with it as she spoke and the hole burgeoned. Squeamish, my tummy flipped over. I forced my line of gaze upwards, concentrating instead on her impressive ropes of hair. 'It tends to be more about them wanting to go home than any specific problem with the foster carer.'

Claire nodded. 'Taylor's desperate to come home. I've told her it shouldn't be too long, now that I've made the break –'

Maisie held up her hand, the sleeve of her blouse rolling back to reveal bundles of multi-coloured twine tied around her wrist. 'You shouldn't have told her that. As I said the other day, you'll need to complete a "Staying Strong" course and a psychiatric evaluation as well.'

Claire chewed away at the inside of her mouth. 'I don't understand why they can't come back now I've left him. My support worker at the refuge says a large family room might become available in the next few weeks. They've said they might be able to hold it for me if you –' Claire's voice trailed to a whisper, her eyes fixed on the thick black lines Maisie was drawing across the page in front of her. It was as if the social worker was underlining her opposition to the reunion.

When Maisie looked up, her eyes were ablaze. 'Nick wasn't the only problem though, Claire, was he? Are you forgetting Reece's leg injury? And that wasn't the only time you've hurt them, was it?'

Claire looked startled, staring into Maisie's face with a look of disbelief. 'I already explained that to you the other day. I thought you understood! I would never deliberately hurt Reece, *never*. But Nick told me that if I didn't sort him out, he would do it himself.'

Maisie was regarding Claire with an unfriendly, sceptical expression and so she turned to me, clutching the edge of the table as she spoke. I could see she was desperate to get her point across. 'He did it all the time – giving me ultimatums – either I punished the kids or he would do it himself.' She began to pant as she spoke, her eyes filling with tears. Suddenly the riddle of the relationship between her and the children made sense, to me at least. Maisie was still wearing a dour, disbelieving look. 'I always tried not to hurt them too much, but it had to be hard enough to satisfy him, or he'd do it all over again.' She began sobbing then, covering her face with the tissue.

I tried to swallow away the lump in my throat, convinced that Claire was as much a victim as her children. Hers wasn't the most appalling story I'd ever heard, but something about Nick's cold-hearted manipulation chilled my blood. I felt sick to my stomach at the thought of a mother being coerced into hurting her children in such a premeditated way; it seemed so much more disturbing than a spur of the moment, hot-headed smack.

Claire shot me a grateful look and then carried on, telling me the compromises she had made to try and keep her children safe. 'You're looking at me and wondering why I didn't just pack up our things and walk out, aren't you?'

My breath caught in my throat, surprised by the direct question. 'Um, well,' I said, trying to say something reassuring, but that was exactly what I'd been thinking.

'It's like telling someone not to eat, you know? For years, staying with Nick was the only way I knew how to live. Now, leaving is the only way to keep us all alive. But I was stuck – Nick swore he would kill us all if I ever walked out on him. He'll go crazy when he finds out I've gone, believe me. There's no way he'll rest until he finds us,' Claire was speaking directly to Maisie now, eyes bulging, voice urgent. 'That's why the kids need to be with me. We need to get right away from here before the police let him out.'

I couldn't help visualising Nick's horror when he discovered that his long reign of terror was over. He was a bully and he was about to get his comeuppance. Slightly ashamed of my vengeful thoughts, I pushed him from my mind.

Maisie tipped sugar from a silver-spouted glass container into her mug, a flicker of unease crossing her face. 'There are measures we can take to protect you,' she said in a monotone, without looking up. 'I expect your support worker has spoken to you about that. We've offered to help you for years, Claire. This hasn't come out of nowhere.'

'But Nick told me that if I ever told anyone the truth he'd go to court for custody. He said there's no way I'd get the kids with my depression as bad as it was. He was never like that in front of anyone else, you see. And it's true; there were times when I felt like I couldn't cope. He'd take them to the park to give me a bit of a breather then. I know it sounds weak but I loved him, I hated him and I needed him, all at the same time.'

Listening as Claire revealed the intimate details of her life felt a bit voyeuristic. I felt so many conflicting emotions as she went on with her story – pity, anger, disgust – that it was difficult to summon a neutral expression. Unsettled, I focussed my eyes on a pot filled with an assortment of sauce sachets. Maisie stirred her coffee with a spoon. 'But *he's* the reason you weren't coping,' she said, sounding irritated. 'He's not your rescuer, Claire.'

'I know that. I do know that. But if someone tells you black is white and white is black enough times, you end up believing it.' Claire shifted in her seat and turned to me. 'When I first met him, he was wonderful,' she said.

Maisie sighed, all but rolling her eyes. Pandering to abusive men was a path worn well by far too many women and I got the impression that the social worker had heard the same thing too many times. 'He was kind and loving; always there whenever I needed him.' Claire stared blankly at the dark coffee in front of her, still untouched, and heaved a sigh. 'It was soon after we got married that things changed. He began to criticise me, subtly at first, but soon I felt as if I couldn't do anything right. And then he started giving my friends the cold shoulder, so much so that I was too embarrassed to bring them home.'

I nibbled the skin on the end of my thumb as I listened.

'Gradually I lost contact with them; I'd lost a lot of confidence and was scared to meet them behind his back. When I got pregnant with Taylor it got much, much worse. The odd shove turned into a punch, but I was alone, no friends, no family, so I clung to him more.'

'Abuse often gets worse during pregnancy.' Maisie's face contorted as she spoke, as if she had a painful ulcer in her mouth that she was trying to protect with her tongue. 'A woman's focus changes and some men feel as if their property is being invaded.'

I had no idea whether my instincts were correct, but it suddenly struck me that, for Maisie, this was personal. I remembered reading some research claiming that some social workers were drawn to their job through experiences of childhood trauma. 'It's not unusual for midwives to have to call security to remove men from the delivery room because they can't bear anyone to get near their partner.'

I shook my head but Claire didn't seem at all surprised.

'Some women even ask for a termination because their partners can't bear the thought of another being inside their bodies.' Maisie was telling me all of this. Whenever she glanced at Claire her expression changed. It was subtle, masked in cool politeness, but I sensed it and I think Claire did too.

She kept her head down as she spoke, occasionally turning to speak to me. 'Nick wouldn't let me breastfeed, not even for the first few days. And then, with Bailey, he said I was spoiling him whenever I picked him up. He was madly jealous of him, even more so than with the girls.' Claire stared off into the distance, as if trying to make sense of it all. 'The only time I could hug him was when Nick went out. Taylor had to see to him the rest of the time. When she was at school, Bailey stayed in his cot.'

My heart lurched at the thought, and Claire's eyes pooled with tears.

'After Taylor was born the years passed in a sort of daze. With the kids around I spent most of my day trying to appease him.'

'Taylor told Rosie that things had deteriorated recently.' Maisie looked at me. 'Isn't that right?'

I nodded, feeling like a tell-tale.

'So what changed?' Maisie demanded with a steely glare. 'What made you suddenly start standing up to him?'

Claire, who had been lifting her cup to her lips, paused, then glanced away, her drink abandoned on the table in front of her. There was a reason; she just wasn't ready to disclose it yet. 'His punishments were getting more and more extreme,' she said, her eyes shooting briefly back. 'I had to hit them harder and harder to satisfy him.' Her lips twisted in shame.

Maisie stirred her coffee, eyes on the cup. 'Abused children become increasingly immune to being punished. They drive the shock of being assaulted deep inside and so their reaction to pain gets watered down. Abusers don't like that at all, it makes them feel less powerful, so they ramp up the violence and get more and more extreme, trying to coax the same horrified, fearful reaction from their child. That's why injuries get more severe over time.' She finally looked up, fixing her gaze on Claire. 'And why it becomes increasingly dangerous to stay.'

Each of Maisie's words sounded like an accusation and I could see that Claire was tormented by them. Her face crumpled in sorrow. 'I don't know why I stayed so long. It's difficult to explain it to myself, let alone anyone else. Except to say that I was frightened. And I wanted a better life for my children than the one I'd had. My parents split up when I was five and after that it was just one step-dad after another, each more brutal than the last.' Desperate to get her point across, Claire spoke with fevered urgency as she looked between Maisie and I. 'All I've ever wanted is a nice home and a happy family. Nick was the only man who ever seemed to care about me.'

It was then that I felt a strange connection with Claire, and not only as one single mother to another. Like me, her life hadn't turned out as planned, but it wasn't just that, not really. It was as if I knew her more intimately than I knew my best friend, even though we'd only just met. I had cradled her baby in my arms after all, listened to her daughter breaking her heart, and I strongly suspected it was her blood I had seen arcing across her bedroom wall.

Although my own separation from Gary had been nowhere near as traumatic, I recognised her longing for what was now lost to her – the conventional family life she had probably dreamed of when she was young. There were times when I had felt that loss keenly and I knew that it wouldn't have been easy to finally accept that the happy family home she had imagined was no more than an elusive fantasy crumbling before her eyes.

From the way she spoke, I got the feeling she was directionless without Nick at her side – he may have been her abuser but he was also her linchpin. As far as I was concerned, it was admirable of her to make such a shattering choice, to sacrifice the family life she'd always dreamed of for the sake of her children.

I was tempted to reassure her that her future would be better than her past, that a happy family life was not lost to her. It would be different from the conventional picture she had in her head but no less fulfilling. I wanted to tell her, most importantly of all, that she'd made the right choice for her children, and therefore ultimately for herself.

'So, I have some news about Nick that I need to tell you about,' Maisie said smoothly, before I got round to countering her. Claire looked up sharply as Maisie closed her pad and steepled her fingers together, hands resting on the cover. 'He was released on police bail early this morning.'

Claire gasped.

'It's OK. He's been told that he'll be arrested if he's found anywhere near his former home and a homicide prevention officer is going to visit the refuge to tell you how to keep yourself safe.'

Claire's eyes had gone wide and my own stomach rolled. Homicide prevention officers – I had no idea they even existed. With no softness in her tone, Maisie went on to tell

Claire that the weeks following a woman's escape from a violent partner were usually the most dangerous and that the children were better off distanced from the situation.

'Where is he?' Claire whispered. She looked panicked.

'He's given police his brother's address in Manchester, but that doesn't necessarily mean he's there. He's asked for contact with the children so there's that to organise, though it will be subject to him passing a psychiatric evaluation. Obviously it will be separate from yours, Claire, there's no question about that.'

Claire had covered her mouth with her hand. When she looked back at Maisie something had shifted in her eyes. She returned the social worker's cold stare with surprising calm. 'He'll be after us, right this very minute, he'll be looking.' She didn't let her gaze waver, not for a second. 'You can't let him near the children. You *can't* let that happen.'

Maisie looked at her and frowned. After a few moments she asked, 'Why not?'

Claire's eyes flitted from me to Maisie, suddenly cloudy with indecision. I got the impression she was weighing up her options.

'Why not, Claire?' Maisie leaned forwards. For the first time, there was kindness in her tone.

Claire bit her lip. 'Swear to me you won't take them away from me permanently,' she said, gripping the edge of the table with gloved fingers. Anticipating something significant, I felt my heart rate picking up.

'I can't do that, Claire. You know I can't.'

Claire gritted her teeth. 'You can't let him see them, OK? Especially not Taylor, you just can't.'

Maisie raised her eyebrows. 'He has certain rights,' she said coolly. 'If there's a reason he shouldn't see them, apart from what we already know, you need to make us aware of it.'

Claire sank back in her seat, Maisie watching her intently. Behind us, the waitress began clearing one of the tables. We waited in silence while she piled empty plates and cups in the crook of her arms. When she took them into the kitchen, Claire looked up and began removing her gloves, her eyes shiny with resolve. She seemed to have reached a decision. 'Look,' she said, holding her hands up for us to see, 'Nick did this to me when I tried to get to Bailey the other night.'

Startled, my throat closed tight. Several of her finger-nails were missing; the nail beds bloody and ripped. One of them was yellow, filled with pus. Maisie's eyes widened and for a brief moment they filled with pity. Seconds later she'd recovered, her official, neutral mask back in place. My stomach was still turning somersaults. 'I know he's been violent, Claire,' Maisie said, in a cool, dry voice that wavered only slightly. 'But that doesn't mean he's lost the right to see his children. It was you that struck them, after all, not him.'

'I've explained that!' Claire shrieked, her chin quivering in exasperation. She ran her raw fingers through her hair and then winced, shaking them in the air and then blowing lightly on them.

Torn

'Nick claims that the violence went both ways – that you were both as bad as each other.'

I wanted to interject then, and ask if Nick had ever been in fear of his life, as I suspected Claire had been, many times. Reminding myself that foster carers were supposed to remain neutral, I bit down on my lower lip.

'I only fought back when –' she broke off, let out a breath and looked around the cafe, angry tears welling up.

My mind ran back over what she'd said about being forced to hurt the children. Who could say that hitting them had been child abuse on her part, and not child protection? Her actions were misguided, perhaps, but not malicious. She didn't strike me as a naturally aggressive person, quite the opposite in fact. For years she had endured abuse at his hands, keeping silent, and yet suddenly she began to fight back. Something else had entered into the equation, I was sure of it. And then I had another thought. 'Reece mentioned something to me last night,' I said slowly.

Claire's eyes snapped over to me. Maisie inclined her head, watching me with interest.

'He said that his father used to like Taylor, but then he stopped.'

I saw the colour drain from Claire's face, her skin fading from pink to sickly white within the space of half a second. Elbows on the table, she buried her face in her hands. There was a long, uncomfortable silence. 'Oh, what difference will it make now? I may as well tell you everything.' Her hands fell away from her face and she took a deep breath. 'Nick started having an affair with my mother when I was pregnant with Taylor.'

I goggled at Claire but Maisie merely nodded as if it was old news. 'That's the reason you're estranged from her isn't it?'

'Yep,' Claire said grimly and glanced at me. I was still shaking my head, I couldn't help myself. Claire didn't seem to mind; she held my gaze and nodded several times, as if to say, yes, can you believe my own mother did that to me? I couldn't. 'Well, they're still at it, on and off, as far as I know. At first I was sick to my stomach, but over the years I managed to anaesthetise myself to it.'

'Oh, Claire,' I said. I couldn't help it. I was still reeling, staggered that anyone could tolerate betrayal on such a scale. But when Claire spoke again, I realised that everyone has their line in the sand; that even the most timid of us snap when we're pushed too far. 'When I was pregnant with Bailey, Nick started to talk about a friend of his who had slept with three generations of the same family. Apparently it's a sort of club some men try to get into, a bit like the Mile High Club, only much, much sicker. Nick was impressed by it, fascinated. Wouldn't leave the subject alone.' She paused. Maisie stopped twirling the end of the pen in her mouth. She withdrew it slowly and made a small sound in her throat, as if everything suddenly made sense.

I continued to nod, my mind still reeling from the horrifying thought of a mother sleeping with her daughter's husband. Was there a great-grandmother involved as well? But then, as the fog in my mind began to clear, a strange

Torn

numbness crept through me. 'Taylor?' I asked in a faint voice. I knew from courses I had attended that the biggest predictor of child sexual abuse was domestic violence and in 70 per cent of cases, where a mother is being abused, her children are suffering alongside her in the worst way imaginable. I felt as if I'd been punched in the stomach.

Claire nodded, looking queasy.

I took a few moments to let this latest revelation sink in. 'Does Taylor know anything of these plans?'

She looked shocked. 'No, course not. I would never have let him involve her. I told him that he'd have to kill me first.'

Remembering Taylor's strange reaction when I had asked her about her grandmother, I twisted my lips and stayed silent. After a few beats Claire said hurriedly: 'She doesn't know any of it, honestly. He said a few things to her, that was all, and tried to make her wear stuff she felt uncomfortable in' – Maisie sucked in a sharp, angry breath – 'but I did my best to stop it,' Claire rushed on defensively, 'that's why things got so bad between us. He went on and on at Taylor to dress the way he wanted and to do her hair and make-up, trying to control her like he did me. That's why she's so obsessed with her looks I think – he made her paranoid. He just wouldn't leave her alone.'

Another little piece of the jigsaw fell into place and my heart squeezed when I thought of the pressure Taylor had been under. Maisie's eyes went cold and she drew herself up, sitting ramrod straight in her chair. She scribbled something in her notebook, her countenance growing increasingly hostile by the second. Oh dear, I thought, pretty sure I knew what was coming. Having admitted that she knew Taylor was directly in harm's way, there was an unhappy inevitability about the outcome. I could tell from Claire's hopeful look that she had no idea what she'd just done. 'You knew he had plans of that nature and yet you still stayed?' Maisie was shaking her head. 'I'm afraid there's no way I'll be able to convince anyone that you're capable of safeguarding the children, not now.'

On hearing that Claire began to pant, her hands clutched to the sides of her head as if trying to stop her hair flying away in a strong wind. There was undoubtedly love there – it was etched onto her features as she tried to absorb the news that she might have lost her children for ever. My heart went out to her, but by staying with their father she had left the children vulnerable to abuse, no matter how many plans she was making to leave. I thought about Millie, a little girl of three who had been left in bed while her mother popped to see her friend who lived a few doors away. Thankfully, when a fire tore through the kitchen of her home, neighbours noticed the smoke and raised the alarm. Millie was placed with a fellow foster carer and when we met her we shuddered, thinking about what might have been. When little ones are involved, a single error of judgement could have devastating consequences.

'I had been trying to leave,' she said in a high voice, crying openly. Exposing such intimate horrors to strangers can't have been easy and again I felt desperately sorry for her. In her own way, she had tried to protect her children. Tears rolled down her cheeks, swollen eye sockets bulging.

Torn

The elderly lady on the other side of the cafe took surreptitious glances towards our table, jaw hanging slack. When our eyes met she looked quickly away, examining her tea. 'I hid money inside packets of dog food, under the floorboards, in the freezer – anywhere he wouldn't find it, but I needed more time. Whenever he went near Taylor I stood up to him. There's no way I was going to let that happen. I told him time and time again, over my dead body.'

Maisie's eyes flicked to mine and set her jaw. 'You've given me no choice, Claire. I'll be speaking to my manager about this but I'm pretty sure we'll be seeking a Full Care Order.'

Claire's arms slid from the table to her lap, visibly trembling as she wept. It was the first time I had ever seen someone so filled with despair. Eventually she looked at Maisie, her face set with determination. 'Yes, I stayed when I should have left, I know that now, but I only did it to protect us all. I love my children, Maisie. I'll do anything to –' she stopped, her voice cracking. Tapping her forefinger on her lips, she gathered herself again. 'You have to believe me,' she said, imploring. 'I'd walk through fire to protect them.'

After the meeting I drove home in a daze, still reeling after the impact of Claire's revelations. In the coming days, as the depth of Claire's and her children's suffering truly hit me, I was overcome by waves of conflicting emotions: sadness, pity and torrents of rage.

It wasn't until several weeks later, as the summer holidays neared, that fear lodged itself in my mind, convinced as I was that Nick Fielding was going to come after us.

Chapter Twenty-Two

The next few weeks passed peacefully enough. Amazingly, after Taylor had missed out on takeaway food as a punishment for refusing to leave school, it never happened again. For some reason, she didn't report the incident to Maisie either. In some ways I think perhaps she was as relieved as the rest of us that someone had finally taken control. Miss Cooper reported that the interaction between Taylor and her peers seemed to have improved, information borne out by an invitation to a cinema party from one of her classmates. It was a perfect demonstration that being nice paid off and I could have cheered when she told me. Of course, Taylor predicted that the film was certain to be 'rubbish', but I think she was secretly thrilled to be included.

All three children had been seeing their mother twice a week at a contact centre several miles away, and although I hadn't seen Claire since our meeting in the cafe, contact supervisors told me that the sessions were going well.

Torn

Despite Maisie's initial pessimism, she reported that Claire had passed her parenting assessment and, though depressed, had been found by two psychiatrists to be otherwise mentally well. Considering what she'd been through, I thought that was a remarkable feat in itself. Things were looking so positive, in fact, that the local authority had changed its plan: instead of seeking a Full Care Order, they were going to request a Supervision Order at the final hearing, which was scheduled for the end of July.

If the judge granted a Supervision Order, the children would be able to return to their mother's care. She would no longer share parental rights with the local authority, but social workers would oversee her care and offer advice where they felt it was needed. Claire, though she was still living at the refuge, had found work and was making plans to find a home for them all. Needless to say, Taylor was thrilled. The two boys, being younger, were less desperate to return home, but Reece got caught up in the excitement when Taylor spoke about what their new house might be like, and it seemed as if they might move on before the end of the summer.

But two weeks into July, just a few days before the children were due to break up for the long summer break, Maisie called with some devastating news. 'So, the legal team have switched back to the original plan. We'll be going for a Full Care Order at the final hearing and reducing contact significantly in the interim.' I was silent for a moment, still trying to absorb it all.

According to Maisie, Nick had been arrested outside the refuge after trying to force his way in. Claire, insistent that she hadn't revealed her whereabouts, appeared to be traumatised, but Nick had a different story, telling police that his wife had pursued him and was desperate to get him back. 'She just couldn't stay away,' Maisie said in a weary tone. It seemed she had been right about Claire all along, although I could tell that the revelation gave her no pleasure.

'But what if she's telling the truth?' I asked, although even I had to admit that it seemed unlikely.

'No one else knew where she was, Rosie,' Maisie answered. 'There's no way he could've tracked her down. Anyway, the kids need to be told about our change of plan. I'll pop round about five, if that's all right with you?'

I spent the rest of the afternoon dreading the moment when they found out the news. Bailey, sensing my nerves, whined every time I put him down, only happy when I sat beside him to play with his garage and cars or carried him around on my hip.

Just after five o'clock Maisie came over as promised, her skin an ashen grey. I felt sorry for her then. We may not have seen eye to eye on the complexities of disciplining children, but she cared deeply about their welfare, that much was obvious. Imparting bad news was one of the tasks I didn't envy social workers of, although, inevitably, it was foster carers who were left to pick up the pieces afterwards.

Taylor and Reece both sensed something was wrong when Maisie told them she had some news. They sank down on the sofa in unison, as if their sides were magnetised, and sat rigidly upright, hands almost touching at the sides. Bailey, still clingy, whined at my side and so I picked him up and put him in his highchair in the kitchen for his tea. I could hear the low, drawn-out murmur of conversation as I laid some finger foods on Bailey's tray, but I couldn't make out what Maisie was saying.

When I went back into the living room to offer them drinks about twenty minutes later, it seemed that Reece had taken the news in his stride. Maisie was silently leafing through the pages of an A5 notebook and as soon as he caught sight of me Reece asked if he could have a biscuit. Nodding placidly when I told him that dinner was nearly ready, he pottered over for a hug and began a game of peek-a-boo with Bailey, who was back on my hip.

The look of anguish on Taylor's face, though, made me feel sick with sadness. With the threat of tears pressing, I patted Reece on the head and then turned briskly away. Later, while the children ate their dinner (with the TV on in the background as a distraction – it was one of those occasions when I was only too happy to break the rules), Maisie and I went outside in the back garden for a private chat.

'Taylor took it well I thought,' Maisie said, with a look of relief. Some colour had returned to her cheeks and her eyes had lost their anxious slant. 'I expected tantrums but she seemed quite chilled about it.'

'Hmm,' I said doubtfully. 'We'll see.' Taylor, disdainful of tears or any outward show of vulnerability, often referred to herself as a tough cookie. If she was going to react, it would be later, when she was alone. 'What's going to happen now, with contact and everything?'

Maisie sighed. 'We can't reduce contact without agreement from the court, so we'll have to wait for the final hearing for that. But Claire's been moved to a refuge miles away so it'll be difficult to facilitate anyway. It means either her or the children travelling a long distance, and all because she was too weak to stay away.'

'What about Nick?'

'We've finally got the psych report back from the evaluation he submitted a while ago.' The social worker scratched her head. 'Nick has a personality disorder with psychopathic tendencies. There's no way he's ever going to have contact with those children again.'

My stomach clenched then, and not only because it was unsettling to hear that the children were closely related to a psychopath. At the LAC review, Nick had announced that if he couldn't have his children, no one was going to have them. 'Does he know that yet?' I asked Maisie, trying to swallow down a rising discomfort.

'I'm meeting with him tomorrow,' she said with a grimace. 'I've arranged to have security with me when I tell him.'

Before she left I told Maisie about my fears that Nick would try to find his children but she reassured me that there had been no lapses in protocol at the office – our whereabouts were confidential and would never be breached. 'But he knows where the children go to school,'

I had said. 'All he has to do is wait outside and then follow us home.'

Maisie had paused for a moment, licking her lips. 'Staff at the school have been told to keep a lookout for him and there's a restraining order banning him from going anywhere near there. But if you're ever worried, just call 999.'

She had been trying to reassure me, but as I watched her walk down the path I was overcome with an unexpected jolt of panic, as if I'd just remembered that I'd left an upstairs window open and a toddler was playing up there.

Within minutes the idea that struck me had galvanised, fixing itself so securely in my mind that I wondered how on earth it had only just occurred to me – Nick wasn't going to let his family disintegrate before his eyes. He was a man who would insist upon having the last word.

Back in the living room, Reece was sitting on the sofa with Bailey curled up on his lap. Captivated by the *Teletubbies*, he shrugged when I asked where his sister was, his eyes fixed on the screen. Eventually I found Taylor upstairs on her bed, her face buried under her duvet so that only her eyes and the top of her head were visible. It was only 6 p.m. but I decided to leave her there for a while; her mind had chosen to distance itself from the painful news and I wasn't going to question that wisdom.

She slept through Bailey's bath time and when I took him into the living room to say goodnight to everyone, there was still no sign of her. Emily and Jamie made their usual fuss of the toddler, planting kisses on his cheeks and playing peek-a-boo under his blanket. Reece joined in with the fun, and after settling Bailey in his cot, I left him playing board games with Emily and Jamie, and went upstairs to see Taylor.

There was a low grunt in answer to my tap on her door so I went in and perched on the edge of her bed. Curled up on her side with her back towards me, she was cradling her new laptop against her tummy, her hand draped protectively over the top. I'd only ever seen them in the shops before, and imagined it was quite expensive. It was a gift that her father had asked Maisie to pass on to her a week earlier, another item that I didn't feel was particularly appropriate for a girl of her age. Her eyes were closed tight, barely flickering when I asked how she was feeling.

'Mmn-mn-mmn,' she said, shrugging.

I waited there for a few minutes, listening to the low tick of her alarm clock. 'Haven't you got washing up or something to do?' she asked irritably, half opening one eye and turning around.

'I have, but I'm not worried about that. I'm worried about you.'

I expected a caustic reply but her only response, as she turned away again, was a heavy sigh. Reaching out, I touched her arm, gently at first, but then I squeezed to convey the message that I was on her side. She lifted her head, twisted it to look at me then sat up and burst into noisy tears. I took one of her hands in mine and ran my thumb across her fingers. 'That came as a bit of a shock, honey, didn't it? I don't think any of us were expecting it.'

She took loud hitching sniffs, trying to stop herself crying so that she could say something. Every time she opened her mouth though, she was overwhelmed by fresh paroxysms of tears. 'It's all my fault, Rosie,' she eventually managed to croak. 'Everything, it's all because of me.'

'You mustn't think like that, honey,' I said, my tone firm, but I wondered exactly how much she knew about her father's plans. Maybe, instinctively, she had sensed his grotesque intentions. Her reaction when I had asked about her grandmother floated into my thoughts again, but it would have been wrong of me to force the issue and ask her about it. Instead I said: 'Your mum and dad are adults. I know you love them, but you're not responsible for their behaviour, not one tiny little bit. There's nothing you could have done to stop all of this.'

'Maisie said that if the judge agrees with her, we'll be going into long-term care. Is that true?'

'Well I think it's a bit early to be worrying about that. We have no idea what the judge will decide.' The legal ruling depended, almost entirely in fact, on the advice given by the court guardian, an official appointed by the court to represent the wishes of the children. I knew that Taylor and Reece had been visited at school by their guardian and, though they hadn't said much about it to me, I assumed they had made it clear that they wanted to return to their mother's care. Why on earth had Maisie told them they might be in care for the rest of their childhood? The children had a right to know about decisions made on their behalf, but sometimes I felt there was wisdom in filtering the whole truth, drip feeding it in small, absorbable chunks and then only when absolutely necessary.

'If that happens can we stay with you?' She was looking at me hesitantly, her chest still heaving with sobs that were straining to break free. My heart twisted in sympathy.

'Well, we'd have to discuss that as a family, but we don't even know what's going to happen yet.'

'I want to stay with you and Emily and Jamie,' she said, her voice rising in a hysterical sob.

Taken aback and touched, I smiled and rubbed her arm. 'That's nice,' I said, 'but let's wait and see what happens first OK?'

She nodded and wiped her nose with the palm of her hand, fingers splayed upwards. 'OK,' she said with a loud, snotty sniff. Wincing, I pressed a tissue into her hand. She shook it out, twirled one of the ends into a point and rammed it up one of her nostrils.

I reeled my chin back. 'Urgh, Taylor!'

Shaky and pale, she choked a giggle and pressed the tissue to her face. Despite everything, I was still able to make her laugh.

Taylor was reserved the next morning, barely uttering a word on the way to school. Reece was his usual inquisitive self during the journey, quizzing me on the make and model of each passing vehicle. Later that day though, when he was sitting at the small nest of tables in the living room doing his homework, his pencil broke in two. Cheeks reddening, he suddenly threw his head back and howled, sounding every bit like an animal in terrible agony. I flew to his side. 'What is it, Reece?' I said, trying to wrap my arms around him.

'Get away!' he screamed, windmilling his arms to ward me off. Tears rolled down his cheeks. 'You're not my mummy! You never lay with us on the grass and watch the stars like Mummy does! You won't even let us snuggle in your bed!'

'I know, honey, I know. There are some things I'm not allowed to do as a foster carer, but I do care about you and I want to help. Come here, love.'

'No! Get away from me.' He stood, kicked the chair over and ran upstairs to his room, sobbing. Taylor, who had been watching silently from the sofa, gave me an acid look, as if the upset was my fault.

Five minutes later he was at my side in the kitchen, looking up at me with his face streaked with tears. 'Someone looks like they need a hug,' I said, cupping his chin. He rushed forward and buried his face into my cardigan, his damp cheek warm on my chest.

Chapter Twenty-Three

'It's the perfect solution,' said my friend, Helen the next day, after hearing that I was feeling a little 'hemmed in' with the children. That's how I'd described it to her, but in truth I was still afraid that Nick might somehow discover our whereabouts. Knowing that I would do anything to find my own children if I'd been told that I would never see them again, I was certain that Nick would do *something*. 'The first guests aren't booked in until the third week of August and if you take some bits and pieces with you, it'll save me a trip all the way up there. You'd be doing me a favour, honestly.'

I first met Helen when we worked together years earlier, in those long forgotten days before children. Single and childless, she loved hearing about my lively home life, but always looked slightly panicked if ever confronted with the children in the flesh. Of course I never revealed any specific details about them, but even the most general overview rendered her breathless. 'Oh God, I can think of nothing worse,' she had said when I first told her about my wish to foster, flapping one hand in front of her face as if she were suddenly hot.

'Well, if you're sure you don't mind,' I said, cheered by the thought of getting away. Helen had recently invested in a tumbledown cottage on the Isle of Islay in the Inner Hebrides of Scotland. As a high-flying executive, Helen was tied to working long hours and though she mightn't get the chance to spend much time there, I think the cottage offered a sanctuary for her to escape to, even if only in her mind. 'I've had the kitchen fixed up and new carpets fitted, but it'd be great if you could work a little bit of magic with the rest of the place.'

It was Saturday, the last weekend before the children were due to break up from school. With the final court date looming, it had been difficult to distract them from worrying about the outcome and the stress was taking its toll. Reece had started having nightmares again, about monsters, dark shadows in his room and a recurring one that involved faceless strangers snatching him from bed (it wasn't hard to work out where that one came from, after Maisie's comment about long-term care). The tummy aches returned with a vengeance as well, turning his face green and his eyes droopy. It broke my heart to see him so anxious, especially since he seemed to have conquered so many of his fears in the weeks preceding social services change of plan.

The news seemed to have completely knocked the stuffing out of Taylor. On the upside, she was less antagonistic, but (and I never thought I'd hear myself say it) somehow I missed her vigorous, loud presence. She still flared up when I least expected it, receiving a week-long computer ban for tearing up several of my favourite books. It was sad to see her so flat, so teary. After promising Helen that I would do my best to make the cottage homely and get it ready for her first paying guests, I put the phone down and swept Bailey up into my arms. A couple of weeks away might be just what the children needed to keep their minds occupied.

When I announced the news to the children Bailey applauded, a look of delight on his face as he stared round at us all. Emily, Jamie and Reece all cheered, the boys breaking into an excited, spontaneous play fight. 'Oh my God-t! Where the heck is Islay?' Taylor asked, looking aghast. 'I've literally never heard of the place.'

I had come to expect violent disapproval from her, so that wasn't a surprise, but another emotion was lingering in her expression as well. Perhaps it was insecurity – I wasn't sure how well travelled the children were – but another part of me analysed it as fear.

'The Isle of Islay. It's a Scottish Island. And we'll be Helen's very first guests in the cottage. How exciting is that?'

'It's huge! It's massive! It's crazy!' Jamie shouted before Reece's arm shot out and yanked him into another tussle. Strictly speaking, play fighting wasn't allowed in the foster home, but for young boys of almost the same age, it came to them as naturally as sniffing and giggling about farts.

Torn

'Mooge!' Bailey shouted as he sat on his bottom and tried to pull his shoes on the wrong feet. He was preparing to leave right that minute, bless him.

'I'm absolutely not going anywhere,' Taylor pronounced, shaking her head. 'No way. I'm staying right here.'

I had noticed that she'd stopped saying 'ain't' recently and her double negatives had dried up as well, but instinctively I knew that it wasn't the right time to praise her for it. She hadn't heard the worst of it yet – there was no internet connection at the cottage and no mobile reception either. For a techno-junkie like Taylor, to whom the networking sites and emails were a regular fix of poison that she just couldn't do without, I was sure the news would come as a shock. Her existence was ruled by constant checking of her updates and even when she was absorbed in an activity she would fly up suddenly and race to check her messages as if her life depended on it. With the computer ban still in place, it had been days since she'd had contact with her online friends.

Personally, I felt that the long break could only be of benefit to her. Our fortnight in the cottage would offer Taylor a hiatus from the daily grind, a chance to disconnect from her venomous friends and redefine herself by what really mattered. I was certain that was what she needed. I was also pretty sure that Taylor wouldn't quite see it that way.

The boys spent the rest of the day in a state of high excitement, dragging tennis rackets and footballs from the shed and piling them up in the hall. Taylor, growing increasingly tense by the hour, resurrected one of the habits that had lain dormant for several weeks. My heart sank when, as I stood at the sink washing up, she walked up to me and flicked a forefinger close to my eyes. 'Taylor,' I said warningly, 'how about you play with Bailey while I get dinner ready?'

The toddler was sitting at my feet, tugging on my jeans. Taylor flicked her finger at me again, almost catching my chin, and then leaned down, scooping her brother into her arms. When I leaned into the living room to check on them a few minutes later though, I saw that Taylor had given him the coins from our savings jar to play with. 'Ah,' I said, sweeping one out of his hands just as he was about to slip it into his mouth. 'I don't think so, mister! You can't play with those.' I gave him a wooden spoon to hold instead but he shook his head manically and burst into a fit of noisy sobs, small arms flapping wildly in front of his face.

Taylor flung her arms around him and gave me a reproving look. 'She's such a mean old cow isn't she? There, there,' she said, but there was none of the aggression she had shown towards me in the kitchen. She sounded jaded and far away, as if she'd slipped into a sudden trance. With Taylor, I was used to her emotions jumping around, furious one minute, morose the next, but this was unusual, even for her.

I stood at the threshold of the door and watched her for a moment, sixth sense whispering to me that something was very wrong.

* * *

Torn

Tired though I was, I hardly slept the night before we went away. Every time sleep drew near, a vision of Nick, the man who had ripped his wife's fingernails from their beds and beaten his daughter black and blue, flashed before my eyelids and jolted me awake. Was I overestimating the risk, I wondered. I had a tendency to fixate on certain anxieties and write them into the future as if they were certain to happen, but then again, it seemed unlikely to me that someone with a sense of ownership as powerful as Nick's would nod politely after being told that he'd never see his family again, and then slip quietly and conveniently away.

Just after 5 a.m. I decided to give up chasing sleep and got up, my head ringing. No wonder Bailey's smiles had been so slow to arrive when he first came to me, I mused, as I peered into the toddler's cot. Still soundly asleep but laying widthways so that his head was angled against the bars, he looked so angelic – and so uncomfortable. Reaching down, I shunted him the right way round, nuzzling one of his soft toys against his cheek when he stirred. I shuddered whenever my mind strayed to thinking about what he might have witnessed in his short life.

Over the sound of the kettle coming to a boil, I heard the soft padding of feet. I turned, surprised to see Taylor shuffling into the kitchen, pulling on the cords of her dressing gown. Eyes bloodshot and red, she looked as if she'd been awake all night.

'Morning, honey,' I said brightly. 'Would you like a drink?'

She shook her head, pulling harder on the ties of her gown. Her eyes settled on mine with a look of uncertainty. 'Rosie, can we not go away? I *really* don't want to.'

Discarding the teaspoon I was holding, I stepped forward and leaned my left hand on the worktop, crossing one foot in front of the other. 'What's worrying you, honey?' I asked, watching her carefully. I couldn't have sworn to it, but once again it seemed to me that she was behaving like a cornered animal, more frightened than angry.

'Oh, for God's sake, nothing! I just don't wanna go, OK-er?'

'You didn't want to go to the chocolate factory, or London, or the seaside, but you enjoyed them all when you got there.' I made a move to pat her shoulder but she jerked away. Her expression darkened, nostrils flaring.

In the next room, I could hear Bailey murmuring. He had taken to calling me 'Mama' over the past week or so, something I tried to discourage, since I knew how much trouble it could get me into. Parents often objected to their children using affectionate family names for their foster carers and part of my job was to navigate a gentle path around their feelings. Bailey already had his own family and he was loved. It was sometimes difficult to discourage though, especially when children were so young, but I was eager to avoid stepping on anyone's toes.

Bailey was on his feet and jumping up and down on the mattress of his cot by the time I reached my room, his plump hands clasped around the bars. 'You cheeky monkey,' I said with a chuckle, faintly aware of Taylor effing, blinding and slamming stuff around in the other room. He beamed at me adoringly and my heart was swept away by the sight. I lifted him up and buried my face into his damp, wayward hair, the harsh words from Taylor all but forgotten. I often wished there was a way for fighters in war-torn countries to see in their enemies the toddlers they had once been – there was something about the innocence of young children that rendered everything else trivial.

Chapter Twenty-Four

With a long journey ahead of us, we set off straight after breakfast, Taylor doing her best to delay us with cries of forgotten toothbrushes and hair straighteners. I noticed that she had packed her laptop, no doubt intending to log on as soon as her computer ban ended. I still hadn't plucked up the courage to tell her it was pointless, hoping that the beauty of our destination and the excitement of being away would more than make up for being cast adrift from cyberspace.

It was a beautiful crisp morning, bright and slightly chilly, ideal conditions for travelling, but after barely an hour on the motorway tempers began to fray, Taylor doing her best to turn her hostility into outright mutiny.

'Ow, Rosie, she's jabbing me with her elbow again!' Reece complained. 'And I still feel really sick.'

'OK,' I said soothingly, scanning the dual carriageway for an exit. 'Deep breaths, Reece. I'll pull over as soon as I can.'

Reece heaved in a shaky breath and let out a wail.

'Stupid cry baby, give it a rest will yer?'

'Taylor, leave your brother alone, hon. He's not feeling too good.'

'Yeah, and whose fault's that? None of us wanna go you know. It's not only me.'

'I do want to go!' Reece shouted spiritedly, though his teeth were chattering.

'Me too!' Emily and Jamie carolled.

'Be, be, be!' Bailey cheered, waving his hands in the air.

'But, Rosie, I feel really baaaad.'

Thankfully, I spotted a sign for services half a mile ahead. Veering my Ford into the car park with a screech of tyres, I pulled up at the earliest opportunity and threw my door open like a getaway driver, the car angled across two spaces. Seconds after I had yanked the rear door open Reece threw up, all over my shoes.

'Oops, sorry, Rosie,' he said, gasping.

After a moment's pause I said, 'It's not your fault, sweetie,' noticing that Taylor had brightened considerably. There was a big, satisfied grin on her face. 'I think we'll stop for a while.' I did my best to clean the pair of us up in the car with wet wipes and some antibacterial gel, Taylor heaving theatrically in the background. I was beginning to think it served me right for making a rash, spur of the moment decision to drive halfway across the country with five young children.

'Urgh, you're so disgusting, Reece,' she kept shrieking, holding the back of her hand to her forehead like a heroine of a silent movie about to be strapped to the tracks of a railway line.

Relieved to be free, Bailey raced ahead when I set him down at the entrance, weaving in and out of the aisles of one of the little shops with shrieks of delight. I managed to find a cheap pair of slip-on trainers for myself in a basket outside a shop selling sunglasses and after paying for them we all trudged into the toilets where I gave my feet a good wash and helped Reece into some clean clothes.

'Surely we're going home *now*?' Taylor asked. 'We'll never make it to Scotland with him barfing all over the place.'

'Yes we will,' I snapped. 'We've only got another couple of hours to go and then we'll be in Glasgow.' I had planned to spend a few hours in the city then drive on to Kennacraig, the Scottish hamlet from which we would catch a ferry over to Islay, but it was becoming clear that there was no way we could travel that far in one day, especially with Reece's travel sickness. 'We're going to spend the night in a bed and breakfast and then move on in the morning,' I announced, making it up as I went along.

'Yay! I've always wanted to go to Glasgow,' Emily said supportively.

'Yes, me too,' Reece added, his cheeks still tinged with green.

'Oh God-t,' Taylor grumbled, hanging her head over the sink.

By the time we'd had a drink and a snack in one of the cafes, Reece had regained some colour. I gave him a travel sickness pill, guiltily delighted that the only ones in stock were the type that caused drowsiness.

Torn

Driving out of the car park, Bailey beamed at me from his car seat every time I glanced at him in the rear-view mirror, the perfect antidote to his sister's scowls. I was pleased to see that both he and Reece fell asleep soon afterwards, hopeful that the rest of the journey would be uneventful. I was also praying that it wouldn't be too difficult to find a B&B happy to accept the six of us at short notice.

We'd been driving about an hour when it began to rain hard, heavy droplets obscuring the windscreen so that I had to lean forwards in my seat and squint to make out the road ahead. Feeling vulnerable in the middle lane, I flicked the wipers on full blast and indicated, pulling left with a tight grip on the steering wheel. A dark shape loomed in the rear-view mirror as a van attempted to undertake my Ford. Gasping, I swerved, skidding back into the middle lane. Behind, a horn blared loudly.

'Oh, Christ! She's literally gonna kill us all!' Taylor lamented.

'Give it a rest, Taylor,' I hissed under my breath, the wipers thudding with a frantic, rhythmic squeak. 'You'll wake the boys.' In truth, I wondered again what I'd been thinking. Door to door, the journey was going to take at least five hours, and then when we got there, how on earth was I going to keep them all occupied for a whole fortnight? On the other hand, my instincts were still whispering to me, urging me on. Somehow, it felt safer, heading far away from home.

* * *

'Oh, for fuck's sake, Reece!' Taylor was screaming, her face contorted with rage. 'Can't you even shut it for two minutes?!'

'Fuck, fuck, fuck,' Bailey parroted happily. Taylor snorted, eyes flashing with glee.

'Taylor!' I hissed, glancing apologetically around. It was almost 10 a.m. the next day and on board the ferry bound for Islay, our fellow passengers were stealing surreptitious, slightly wary glances in our direction. The travel sickness pills had worked a treat, the anti-sickness element at least. Reece seemed to have escaped the drowsy side effects though, his excitement increasing with each passing mile. It was wonderful to see him so animated – from what I could gather, the children had only ever been on holiday once before – but his constant chatter was grating on Taylor and several times she'd come close to lashing out.

'Hey, Reece, come and have a look over here,' I said, beckoning him to sit beside me. 'I think those birds are ospreys.'

'Wow!' he shouted, cheeks flushed from his constant babble. He skidded over and leapt onto the wooden bench beside me, his huge gappy smile lighting up his face. Last night his front tooth had finally fallen out and his face looked rounder somehow, cuter than ever. Bailey, clasped tightly on my lap, bobbed up and down as he pointed across the loch. 'Birdie, birdie!' he shouted breathlessly over the rhythmic lap of waves. I had been pacing the deck for the past half an hour, giving him a chance to stretch his legs, but I was too nervous to let him run free with water all around us.

The air across West Loch Tarbert was sweet and cool, saltily fragrant in a light mist. Every now and then the bright July sunshine broke through, glinting across the surface in little eddies of light. After giving Bailey an affectionate squeeze, I pulled out my phone and snapped a few photos of the ospreys perched on passing driftwood.

A shout rose up from the other side of the ferry and then a wave of cheers went round the passengers. 'Look, Mum!' Emily shrieked, waving her hand frantically as she called me over. Jamie was leaning over the side of the boat beside her.

'Awesome!' he shouted and as we raced over to join the crowd we spotted them: a pair of dolphins moving through the water in seeming slow motion, barely twelve feet from the boat. Swinging Bailey around so that he was facing outwards, I hitched him up a little higher so that he could peer over the rail, my arms clamped tightly around his waist.

'Look, Bailey! Dolphins!' Emily cooed, pointing.

The dark shapes submerged, moving silently away, but seconds later they surfaced in tandem, their glistening fins cutting through the ripples and waves. Suddenly they leapt out of the water in a graceful arch, their tails hitting the surface with a breathtaking, colossal splash. A spluttered exhalation rose from the water and into the mist, stray droplets of foamy water catching our faces and making us gasp.

'Are they real?!' Reece asked, jumping up and down on the deck. Beside him, I noticed a look of absolute joy lingering on his sister's face.

'Absolutely,' I said, laughing. The air around us was filled with a tang of fish, sulphur and salt.

'God, you're so thick,' Taylor said disgustedly, shaking her head and clumping off across the damp planks to the other side of the boat. She plonked herself down on the bench, rested her elbows on her knees and slumped forwards, her chin resting in her upturned hands.

'Stay on the bench and don't lean over,' I warned the others and then went to sit beside Taylor, Bailey resting on my lap.

'They might surface again in a minute, Taylor,' I said. 'You'll miss them if you stay over here.'

'What do I care?' she snarled, heaving herself up and slamming herself down with her back towards me. The timber creaked beneath her.

'But you adore animals. I thought you'd love to see them.'

She straightened and twisted her head to look at the water. When she turned back and fixed her eyes on me they were cloudy with rage. 'We're not going to get a signal on the island are we?' she demanded.

I was about to answer when a gull cried overhead, and then an odd sensation gripped me, a sort of ripple of suspicion. Moments later, with a slap of waves on the hull, it was gone. 'I don't suppose we are, no. But you won't miss out on your calls with Mum, OK? We'll find a payphone for you to use, I promise.'

'Then we're dead, Rosie, do you realise that?' she said in a flat tone. 'We're basically all dead.'

As we neared Port Ellen harbour the column of arched windows in the white-washed facade of Carraig Fhada lighthouse came into view and my spirits lifted. Arriving felt like an accomplishment in itself and it was such a relief that our journey was almost over. Several adorable double-fronted houses stood side by side along the shoreline, just visible beyond the moss-covered rocks. It was such a cosy welcome sight that I immediately relaxed. Riveted by the stunning views across the picturesque seaside village and the sharp, fresh smell of seaweed and salt, we lingered on the upper deck of the ferry before venturing below for our car.

By the time we reached the front of the queue to disembark, it was nearing 1 p.m. and the children were exhausted. Eyelids drooping, they leaned towards each other in the back of the car, heads leaning sideways like baby birds. Taylor, though her eyes were shadowed, sat rigidly upright in her seat like a sentinel on guard, head shooting sharply one way and the other as we drove over the gangplank.

The landscape was overwhelming at first, stunningly beautiful, but so shockingly barren that it almost took my breath away. Lazy oohs and aahs rose from the back of the car when I pointed out the wild goats roaming nonchalantly across the narrow roads, but even Emily was too tired to give much of a reaction. In the boot of my Ford was a crate filled with essentials: tins of food, coffee, tea, nappies and, of course, the obligatory ketchup and Calpol, but I needed milk, butter and a few other bits. It occurred to me, as I drove towards the village of Port Ellen, that I should have done more research before dragging the children out to such a remote part of the country. With the small purposeful voice on a loop in my head, encouraging me to get away, I hadn't even checked with Helen that there was a shop on the island.

It was a relief to see, as we approached the outskirts of town, a small limestone building crowned with a bell tower. Though it looked like an old school, brown sacks of potatoes rested again its sloping, craggy walls, layers of vegetables arranged in wooden crates beside them. There were several other shops as well, including a chemist, post office and bank. I had begun to feel slightly panicky – what if we'd had to return to the mainland, after the mammoth journey we'd already made? When I pulled into the car park, Taylor was incredulous. 'What? We've come all this way and now you're making us go shopping?!'

'We need a few bits, that's all. We won't be long.'

'*I* won't be any time at all. I'm staying here, in the warm.'

'Taylor, it's 18 degrees outside,' I said choppily, 'hardly mid-winter.' Fearing a sit-in, I kept my gaze lowered and forced an exaggerated cheery tone as I lifted Bailey out of the car. 'Come here, my gorgeous boy.'

Still clutching his sippy cup, he held it aloft as I hugged him close. 'Mum-mum-mum-mama,' he cooed, pressing his nose against mine and smacking an unexpected, sloppy kiss right on my lips. Laughing, I set him down on the pavement and let him toddle in front of me towards the shop. In a flash he'd disappeared from sight so I jogged to keep up, hoping that Taylor had climbed out of the car with the others. I could hear several pairs of footsteps following me but kept my eyes fixed straight ahead – turning around to check would have drawn attention to her, possibly igniting a full-blown meltdown. You're getting good at this! I told myself as I caught sight of Taylor's reflection in one of the glass doors. Stalking along behind the others, she poked the magazines on a rack aggressively as she passed by. At least we'd managed to avoid a stand-off though, something I was too tired to cope with just then.

The tiny supermarket had a bygone feel to it and there was something enchanting about the slightly grubby carpet tiles beneath my feet, the old-fashioned metal advertisements stuck along the walls and lopsided, slightly rusting shelves. They looked ancient. Even more appealing, the aisles were mostly deserted, such a strange sight for us, accustomed as we were to negotiating our way through hordes of shoppers.

A sweet, slightly herby aroma rose to meet me halfway along the first aisle, transporting me back to childhood visits to my grandmother's house, where every room seemed to smell of honey and chutney and newly baked bread. I felt instantly at home. Unfortunately, Bailey seemed to share my sentiments.

Admiring its charm as I loaded bread, milk and a couple of packets of biscuits into my basket, I had taken my eyes off him for no more than a second or two. Spinning around, I caught sight of his small feet, standing at the end of the aisle. By the time I reached him he'd managed to drag several packs of toilet paper from the shelves. While sitting proudly on top of one of them, he booted the rest across the carpet-tiled floor. 'Oh no you don't!' I cried, dashing over and crouching in front of him. 'You little rascal!'

Standing behind me, Emily, Jamie and Reece giggled. Taylor joined them, malice and delight dancing across her face. Boosted by his thrilled audience, Bailey began to shriek. Leaning over, he tore gleefully at the plastic covering, trying to free the rolls of paper. 'Oh yes, wouldn't you just love to do that!' I said, bending over and prying them away from him. I could hardly blame the little scamp for creating a bit of mischief after being cooped up for such a long time. 'Tell you what, we'll buy some extra rolls and play a game with them when we get to the cottage shall we?' I said, scooping him up.

Immediately he arched his back and flung his arms over head, wriggling free. 'NO!' he yelled, stamping his feet and then dragging them along as I tried to gain purchase and haul him up into my arms.

'Oooh, look at that,' I said in my most enticing tone. 'Eggs! You love eggs don't you?' It was a pathetic attempt at distraction and he was having none of it. Squawking like an injured animal, he kicked out and thrashed around, desperate to submerge himself back in the middle of the mess he'd made. Emily, Reece and Jamie circled me and tried to distract him but Taylor stayed back, laughing with relish.

With a whooping noise I hoisted Bailey over my shoulder and, clasping his ankles, I lowered him down my back. His screams converted to breathless giggles and when I heaved him back to my shoulder he shouted in my ear, 'Again, again!'

'Later,' I said, laughing and setting him back on his feet. It was then, as I tightened my grip on his hand and turned around, that I saw the colour drain from Taylor's face. Her eyes were fixed on the glass front of the shop, her skin almost yellow in the harsh overhead lights. Following her line of sight, all I could make out was the low rumble of a car engine as a dark 4 x 4 pulled into the car park. Behind, an elderly woman was dragging a small wheeled trolley behind her. 'What is it, Taylor?' I asked. A trace of laughter lingered in my voice but my scalp had begun to prickle.

'Nothing,' she snapped, but she looked terrified. Seconds later she relaxed, her shoulders slumping in relief. I studied her carefully as we made our way towards the ruddy-faced, slightly puzzled looking man at the till.

'Here on holiday, then?' he asked cheerfully as I set the wooden basket onto the counter. It took me a moment to answer. My heart was thudding high up in my chest.

* * *

Baylight Cottage would have been the perfect place to film a BBC period drama. Rose trees flanked its neat wooden porch, wisteria trailed the windows and stretched all around, rugged cliffs overlooking the sea. A ramshackle cobblestone wall surrounded the sprawling gardens, over-shadowed in parts by ferns and brambles. Walking towards the door with Bailey in my arms, I felt as if we had stepped into one of those slightly fuzzy picture postcards of an idyllic country village. It was no wonder that Helen had fallen in love with the place, I thought, trying to distract Bailey from bashing the top of my head with his stubby fingers.

'I love it!' Emily cried, before I'd even unlocked the door. 'I absolutely love it!'

Bailey kicked his legs excitedly and dug his heels into my midriff as I eased a key into the lock, chivvying me along like a jockey riding a reluctant horse. He wriggled from my grasp inside the hallway, capering ahead and bashing flattened hands on one of the closed doors in front of us. Lowering my bag onto the varnished oak floorboards, I caught the faint scent of furniture polish and lavender and was suddenly filled with the sense that the break might not have been such a bad idea after all.

'This place is so coooool!' Jamie shouted, whizzing over to Bailey and opening the dark oak door. Reece bounded after him and Emily slipped upstairs, eager to be the first one to explore the bedrooms.

The living room was a large bright space with peach-coloured walls and two floral, wooden-framed sofas arranged around a huge multi-coloured rug. There were white wooden shutters at the windows and paisley throws dotted here and there. In the middle of one of the longest walls was a wood burner inside an inglenook fireplace, a brass coal bucket beside it on the hearth.

'Where's the TV?' Taylor demanded, hands on her hips. It was the first time she had spoken since we'd left the supermarket.

I paused. Where was the TV? I turned slowly around, scanning the room. In one corner stood a large wooden chest with a music centre and speakers resting on it, but there was no sign of a TV anywhere. Really? What was Helen thinking, I thought, a mild panic setting in. What if it rained for a fortnight? 'Erm, it looks like there isn't one. But hey, listen, it's a peaceful retreat. We don't need a gogglebox intruding on our time together, do we?'

Taylor stared at me in disbelief. Jamie said nothing but stared around the living room, as if I had hidden the television away as some sadistic practical joke. The unfailingly supportive Reece was suddenly lost for words as well. Even Bailey had fallen still. Emily, appearing at the door, looked concerned. 'What's happened?'

'There's no bloody TV!' Taylor answered, hands thrown heavenward in disgust.

Emily gave a slow shrug. As an avid reader, she wasn't too bothered.

'Oh come on,' I said to the others, rubbing their shoulders and trying to jolly them along Julie Andrews style. 'Why the long faces? It'll be great! We'll go fishing and hiking and we'll have picnics on the beach. Who needs TV when you have the great outdoors?'

Reece raised an eyebrow.

'Well *I* think we –' Taylor began, but I interrupted her hurriedly, before she could gather any support from the others.

'So, here's the plan. We're going to have a lovely lunch – we'll all feel better once we've eaten. And then we'll explore the garden. How does that sound?'

Taylor put her lips together and made a loud whizzing noise in mock excitement. 'What? Eat and then pace around a piece of wet grass, all in one afternoon? I'm not sure we can take that much excitement.'

I ignored her and went into a kitchen so delightfully rustic that it was like walking through the pages of a country life magazine. Across one wall there was a cream-coloured dresser, gold-rimmed porcelain plates, cups and saucers arranged along the shelves. Across the top were bunches of dried lavender tied with string, mint, sage and parsley arranged neatly in silver pots along the window sill opposite. There was no electric kettle but I managed to find some matches and a little copper pot to set on the stove. I lit the Aga and boiled some water for coffee, sipping it while I peeled some potatoes. Bailey watched avidly as he sat in front of me on the wooden work top, every so often darting out a hand, grabbing one of the curly peelings and then launching it across the floor with a deep throaty chuckle.

Soon, we all sat around the long farmhouse table in the middle of the kitchen, the children tucking into pie and mash with vigour. It was so deeply satisfying to see Bailey enjoying his food that I barely touched my own until he'd almost cleared his plate.

Later that evening when the children had all gone to bed, I sank back into the deep floral sofa with a loud groan of relief. Luxuriating in the silence, I dropped my head back and closed my eyes. Instantly, a wave of anxiety rushed through me. I straightened, blinking as I tried to identify what was bothering me. And then I remembered – it was Taylor's fearful expression in the supermarket. From earlier training sessions I knew that holidays were a time when bad memories could surface; the unfamiliar environment, qualms about birth parents and disruption of routines all working together to make the joyous occasion stressful. Somehow though, I didn't feel that was the problem with Taylor. Her feelings towards me were complex, I knew that much, but I was pretty certain that she felt secure in my care. She knew she was safe with me.

So what was she so afraid of? For all my lecturing, as I listened to the rain tapping at the window and the creak of pipes as water ran through the heating system, I began to wish for the distraction of television myself.

In my bedroom, with the hooting of owls drifting through the metal-framed windows and foxes calling mournfully to their babies, Taylor's words on the ferry came back to me. Surrounded by the chaos of the day, their impact had been muted but now, with everyone safely ensconced in their respective rooms and the sound of distant waves crashing against the rocks, they reared up on me with a vengeance. It wasn't unusual for her to say disturbing things, but there was something in the expression on her face and the flat inevitable tone in her voice when she said we were all dead, that I found hugely unsettling. Not for the first time, I couldn't rid myself of the sense that an unwelcome presence hovered nearby.

I woke an hour later with an ominous pressing against my chest, as if someone had placed a weight on top of the bedclothes. Moonlight flickered eerily across the floor and, what with the unfamiliar bed and the sense that something was wrong, I doubted that I would get any sleep that night.

Closing my eyes, I tried to conjure a picture of the Port Ellen bay to relax myself. Slowly, the tension drained from my limbs and I drifted towards sleep again. A short length of time later though, instinct woke me. My eyes sprang open and the first thing I saw was a dark shape in my room, hovering by the door. For one terrifying moment, as I sat up and gathered the bedclothes protectively around me, I thought of Nick Fielding. A scream lodged itself in my throat and came out as a whimper. But then my eyes adjusted to the dark, the shape revealing itself as Taylor.

I let the bedclothes fall to my lap and snapped the bedside lamp on. 'Goodness, you gave me a fright! What's wrong, honey?' I asked, reaching for my dressing gown and pulling it on over my pyjamas.

She reacted instantly to the light, drawing back and covering her eyes with the back of her hand.

Torn

'Taylor?' I said warily, kneeling up. I wondered whether she might be sleepwalking, but as I crawled over the mattress towards her she lowered her hand, squinted and then blinked, her eyes clear and alert. I patted the mattress. 'Come here, love. Tell me what's wrong.'

She sat down tentatively, as if she anticipated a prickly landing and then interlaced her fingers and stretched them out in front of her. Reeling them back, she covered her face with her hands, groaned and then linked fingers again, stretching them out so that her shoulders hunched over. A flapping sensation started up in my stomach and fluttered up to my chest. I wanted to grab her shoulders and give her a gentle shake. 'Taylor, I don't know what's going on but, whatever it is, however bad you think it is, you can tell me.'

She turned to look at me and drew in a breath, her brows knotted in an anxious frown. 'Um, oh God, Rosie. I don't know what to do.'

A fuzzy sensation filled my head, like the faraway feeling the day before a cold comes out. I reached for her hand and wrapped my own around it. It was warm in the room but she was freezing. 'There's nothing we can't fix, honey.'

She took another breath and settled her eyes on me again. 'Um, well, it's to do with Dad.'

Heat rushed to my face. 'Right? What about Dad?'

'He's knows where we are.'

Feeling as if I'd been winded, I pressed my hand against the mattress and sat unmoving for a moment, just to get my breath back. It must have been a full half-minute before I found my voice. 'What do you mean? How could he?'

She let out a loud groan. 'I told him! I had to. He said he'd hurt Mum if I didn't tell him everything.'

My mind groped to make sense of what she was saying. 'You've had no contact with your dad though, have you?' But as soon as the words left my mouth the penny dropped. I had policed the use of her mobile, but she could have contacted whomever she wanted online.

'I'm sorry, Rosie. I *had* to. Dad opened a Myspace account in a made-up name and said that if I didn't keep in touch he'd do horrible things. When he found out he couldn't see us anymore he made me give him your address. He said he'd come and get us and take us to Mum.'

'So he knows where we live,' I recapped slowly, the panic settling itself against my voice box. 'But he doesn't know where we are now, does he?'

She looked at me guiltily from the corner of her eye. 'He said that if I ever let a day go by without contacting him, he'd come after us. Then you put me on that computer ban so it's been days since I messaged him. And, Rosie,' she said, her voice rising in panic, 'I think he might have followed us here.' She inclined her head towards the door. 'For a second yesterday I thought I saw his car, at the supermarket.'

Seized by sudden fear, I looked frantically around, as if Nick might be hiding somewhere in my bedroom. My arms and legs trembled.

'I don't think it was him, but what if he did follow us here, Rosie?'

'He'd be crazy to follow us all the way up here,' I said, trying to think rationally. I felt my pulse rate slowing. Of all the places to try and snatch children from, a tiny island only reachable by ferry or helicopter, had to be one of the worst. 'I don't think he'd come here, Taylor, really I don't, so let's calm down, have a nice drink and you can tell me all about it.'

'It's a long story,' she said five minutes later, as she sat next to me on the sofa. After making some drinks, I had checked every window and door in the cottage to make sure they were secure. My mobile phone was in the pocket of my dressing gown, although it wasn't much use – there was no signal. Taylor perched herself on the edge of the sofa, trembling so violently that the surface of the warm milk rippled in the mug balanced on her knees.

'Yes, I expect it is,' I agreed, leaning back against the cushions. 'And we've got all night.'

She bit her lip as she swivelled her gaze to meet mine. 'You're gonna be *so* cross.'

'That's never stopped you before,' I said, raising my eyebrows. I was trying to encourage her to relax and she laughed loudly, a high-pitched, hysterical giggle. I reached out and rubbed her shoulder. 'Seriously though, I won't be cross if you tell me the truth. It's very important that you're honest with me, Taylor, you understand that, don't you?'

She nodded earnestly. 'I don't know what you want to know.'

'Well, how about you start by telling me about this contact with your dad. How long have you been in touch with him? Since you first came to me?'

She twisted her face into a sort of tortured grimace. 'Yeah. Dad said if I did what he told me to, we'd be able to go back home to Mum. He said if I didn't we'd end up living with all different people and probably have to move somewhere hundreds of miles away from them.'

'What did he want you to do?'

'I was supposed to get you to chuck us out,' she said, her voice wobbling. 'He told me to behave as badly as I could so that you couldn't put up with us anymore. He said if I did that no one else would take us and we'd have to go back home.' And then she kept talking, words spilling from her trembling lips faster and faster, as if time were running out. It seemed that her worst tantrums and misdemeanours had been carefully orchestrated by her father. Taylor had been his puppet, dancing to his every command through fear of what might happen if she didn't. 'I'm really so sorry about your photos,' Taylor said, sounding genuinely regretful. 'I felt so bad for doing that.'

I shook my head. 'You didn't know what to do for the best. At least I understand why you did it now. I suppose the sit-ins were his idea as well?'

'The what?'

'You know, refusing to leave school all those times.'

There was a pause then she looked at me guiltily and shook her head. 'That was my idea.'

I raised my eyes to the ceiling. 'Well, I'm sorry you didn't trust me enough to tell me any of this before now.'

She blushed. 'I wanted to, *so* bad. But Dad said he'd find out where you lived and burn your house down if I told you anything. I had to pretend that I didn't know your address. He kept asking me and asking me and I wouldn't say, but then, last week, I had to tell him. He was going to hurt Mum if I didn't.'

I rubbed her leg. 'You've been so brave, telling me all of this.' But as I spoke I realised something else as well. It struck me like an electric shock and the hair on the back of my neck tingled. 'So *that* was how he found out where your mum was staying in the refuge. She didn't tell him after all.'

Straight away, tears appeared on her cheeks. 'I had to tell him. He said he'd track us down and kill us all if I didn't. I hate him, Rosie, I really hate him.' She looked at me, suddenly hesitant, and then she said, 'He said the weirdest things to me'.

With a chill entering my chest, my hand slid from her leg to the sofa. 'What things?' I asked in a tight voice. I tried to keep my expression neutral – the last thing I wanted was for her to clam up.

'Weird, disgusting things,' she shrieked, and then she started to weep. I remembered reading somewhere that giving someone a hug when they're upset can give the impression that the time for talking is over. I reached out for her hand instead, giving it a squeeze. After a few minutes the sobs subsided and she sniffed, wiping her nose with my proffered tissue. 'He told me he liked the way my body was changing,' she said quietly, keeping the tissue in place so that I couldn't see her face. 'He said he wanted me to show it off and that he'd leave Mum alone if I kept him happy. I tried to, Rosie. I wanted to help Mum, but it made me feel like throwing up when he said stuff like that.'

'He should never have said those things, Taylor. That was very wrong of him,' I said, my stomach clenching at the thought of what he might have done to her.

'He was gonna take me to Nan's house. He said she'd let us spend some time together on our own,' she peered at me over the top of the tissue, her face contorting in another sob. 'I really didn't wanna go, though. Why would Nana say that?' she managed to choke out. 'I t-t-thought she l-l-loved me.'

'Oh, sweetie,' I whispered, pulling her into a hug. Laying her head on my shoulder, she let out a breath, her trembling arms tightening around me. Even though it was awful, part of me felt hugely relieved. It sounded to me as if Taylor had escaped the worst of what Nick had planned for her. I rubbed her back and then patted her before pulling away.

'He's never going to leave us alone, is he,' she said, blowing her nose on the tissue. It wasn't a question. Her voice was flat, defeated.

I grabbed her hand and squeezed it. 'He's going to have to, my darling. There's a whole network of people ready to help you, Taylor, and now we know the truth we can sort this out. He's never going to be able to threaten any of you again.'

'Dads are supposed to love their kids aren't they? Why do I have to be so disgusting that even my own dad doesn't want me?' she asked, searching my face with an angry scowl. I got the sense that she was bracing herself for confirmation that she was bad, that it was all her fault.

I stroked her long hair back from her face and touched her damp chin with my thumb. 'Some people don't know how to be good parents, but it doesn't mean they don't love their children. It's nothing you've done, Taylor. You're a wonderful girl. The problem is with your dad, not with you.'

'Do you think so?' She flushed pink.

'Absolutely I do.'

'Why couldn't we just have an ordinary dad like everyone else?'

I gave a little laugh. 'Now there's a question a lot of people around the world have probably asked at some time or another, honey.'

She stared off into the middle distance, thinking. 'I don't think my dad is a nice person at all. I think he's –'

I stopped myself from completing her sentence. The feelings she was bound to feel towards her father were complex. She was going to need lots of time to work them out for herself.

Chapter Twenty-Five

Since there was no signal at the cottage, we drove into Port Ellen before breakfast the next morning to use a payphone. It was raining again and Emily and the others sheltered in a shop doorway while I took Bailey into the old-fashioned red telephone box with me. Eager to bring Maisie up to date, I felt breathless as I waited for the call to connect. When I heard the slow cadence of her answerphone message, my heart sank.

The final court hearing was due to start in less than a week and so Maisie needed to know the truth as soon as possible. Taylor studied my expression avidly as I made my way over, her shoulders hitched almost to her ears. Too tense to go back to her room, I had tucked her up on the sofa under the duvet after our chat, but she'd barely slept more than three hours. Her eyes were heavily shadowed and her skin was pale. She was so desperate for news, bless her. 'I can't get hold of her at the moment,' I said, lifting my hand in a placatory gesture at the sight of her tortured expression. 'But don't worry, we'll find an internet cafe and then I can send Maisie an email.'

'Ooh, ooh, did you say cafe?' Reece said, bobbing up and down. Oblivious to all the drama, he was desperate for some breakfast. Bailey, suspended in a baby carrier fixed to my back, clapped his hands together and then rested his chin on the top of my head, reaching down to pat my cheeks.

'But what if there isn't one?'

I put my hands on her shoulders. 'Listen, honey, we'll get hold of her somehow, I promise. I'll swim if I have to.' Her eyes pooled with tears and she pressed her lips together, nodding gratefully.

MacTaggart Community Cybercafe, a passer-by assured me, was just a five-minute walk away. Taylor led the way down pavement-less roads, almost breaking into a run when the cafe came into view. Inside, I ordered everyone a cooked breakfast and then, after securing Bailey into a highchair beside me, I logged onto to one of the computers. It was difficult to know where to start but I did my best to sum everything up in a succinct email and then clicked send, hoping Maisie would be able to get back to me before the end of the day. My mobile showed that I had a signal so I tried the social worker's number again, giving up when her answerphone message clicked in.

By the time we had eaten the rain had fortified into a downpour and so we spent the rest of the morning swimming at the local leisure centre. Bailey, nervous at first, had clung tightly to my shoulders, but after a while he relaxed, scooping handfuls of water and arching it over his back with excited little shrieks. Taylor remained out of reach, her mind, I guessed, with her mum, hundreds of miles away.

We returned to MacTaggart's for lunch, all of us ravenous after our swim. Leaving the girls to order for me, I logged on to a computer, relieved to find an email from Maisie sent at 9.33 a.m. that morning, barely fifteen minutes after my own email to her. I read it quickly, my eyes scanning the whole message and then returning to the beginning to try and absorb it slowly. Before returning to the table I called Maisie's mobile, my heart sinking when she confirmed what she'd already written.

'But everything's changed,' I said, trying to keep my voice low. I was aware of Taylor staring at me from the other side of the cafe. 'Surely what I told you sheds a different light on things?'

'Not as far as we're concerned. I've checked with senior managers, Rosie, and they're of the same opinion as me. We don't feel Claire is strong enough to stay away from Nick. She's shown time and time again that she's not capable of safeguarding those children. There's no way we can change our plan.'

Taylor raced over when I ended the call. As soon as she saw the look on my face she began crying. 'Now, let's not get too worked up, love,' I said soothingly. I offered her a tissue and she jabbed at her tears. 'It's not their decision that really counts, at the end of the day. It all depends on the judge.'

* * *

Torn

Besides confirming that the local authority was continuing with its plan to obtain a Full Care Order, Maisie told me that Nick was in police custody awaiting a bail hearing. It seemed that on the day we had left for Islay, Nick was up to his old tricks, selling heroin and crack cocaine. It was a relief to know that he was no longer a threat to our safety – I guessed that we'd never know how far he might have taken his threat to hunt us down, although when arrested the police had found a scrap of paper in one of his trousers pockets, our home address scrawled on it. The thought, even now, leaves me cold.

Without the fear of being followed hanging over our heads, I began to relax and enjoy the beautiful surroundings. Reece seemed to have made peace with being away from his birth family, throwing himself into the holiday with as much gusto as Jamie and Bailey. Emily, having brought a pile of books away with her, was her usual happy self and Taylor, though distracted, began to lose that pained expression.

Some of the locals had told us that ghosts from Duntulm Castle on the Isle of Skye, walk the cobblestone paths of Islay when the moon rises. Sensing Taylor's interest, they indulged her with detail, telling her that their ghoulish screams were sometimes heard echoing across the desolate moors, where Islay's legendary smugglers once roamed. Their stories transformed her attitude to walks and she became as keen as the rest of us to explore the island's craggy moors.

That wasn't to say the days were entirely peaceful. Nick may have directed some of Taylor's more disturbing behaviour but, being a feisty character at heart, there were still regular outbursts. Whenever her temper blew, I tried to imagine how torturous it must have felt, sensing what her father had wanted from her. By inhabiting that space, it was easier for me to step back and become a bystander, allowing her to rail against the world until her anger fizzled out.

A week into our holiday, about three days before the final hearing was due to start, Max, the children's guardian, contacted me. 'I'm so pleased to hear from you,' I told him in hushed tones as I pulled on Bailey's reins and drew him away from the others. We had been visiting the museum of Port Charlotte, the older children trying on some ancient-looking clothes. Thankfully, Taylor was so absorbed in tying a bonnet around Emily's neck that she paid me no attention as I spoke. 'Is there any news?'

'Well, I expect you've heard that the local authority is sticking to its plan?'

Bailey spun around in circles, trying his best to break free. Wincing as the reins tightened around my fingers, I released them and caught hold of him, lifting him up with one hand and planting him on my hip. 'Yes, I heard,' I said, moving closer to a display cabinet to distract Bailey with the shiny artefacts. He leaned forward and blew a loud raspberry on the glass. 'And what's your feeling about it all?' I asked. Knowing how much the decision meant to Taylor, I held my breath as I awaited his answer.

'I've met with Claire several times now, and I believe I've come to the right decision. What's your view? In terms of the children, I mean. When I saw them at school they seemed very keen to get back to their mother. Is that your understanding?'

I told him then about the adoring way the children spoke about their mother and their longing for her when they were unwell. Jiggling Bailey on my hip, I relayed their stories of impromptu dances around the kitchen and night-time gazing at the stars. Of course, my personal opinion was of no importance whatsoever, except that, knowing the children as well as I did, I was able to provide another insight into their thoughts and wishes. Anyway, I appreciated being asked.

'Thank you, Rosie. That's helpful. I have to say, I think Claire has a lot to offer the children. I know she's had some issues with depression, but frankly I think that's a natural response to her appalling circumstances as much as anything else. I'm going to oppose the local authority's decision.'

'Down!' Bailey shouted when I stopped bobbing him around and slipped the phone into my bag. As soon as his little trainers touched the floor he hurtled pell-mell towards the others, flinging his arms around Emily's legs. She beamed at him delightedly. Taylor gave me a sharply inquisitive look as I walked over. She was standing in front of a large antique mirror balanced against the far end wall, an ornate lace scarf draped over her hair. 'Who was that?' she asked. She had noticed after all.

Reluctant to give her false hope, I wasn't sure whether to tell her the good news. While it was true that family court judges placed great value on feedback from guardians, the local authority had plenty of evidence to support their claim that their mother was vulnerable. 'No one you need to know about,' I said, playfully nudging her nose between my thumb and forefinger. But it was like trying to steer a toddler away from puddles and after a few minutes of badgering I caved in. 'All right, it was Max, your guardian,' I said, holding up my hand and adding, 'but listen to me. I don't want you to get your hopes up, OK?'

On the day that the final judgment was due, I took the children to a beach known as Singing Sands, partly because it was recommended to us by locals but mainly because Taylor was literally sick with nerves. I wanted to take her somewhere absorbing and keep her mind occupied so that she wouldn't fret so much. It was a beautiful day, one of the first since we'd arrived, and I couldn't help hoping that the clear skies and bright sunshine were some sort of benediction.

As soon as the beach came into sight Reece and Jamie were off, zigzagging across the sand in two different directions. Bailey toddled first after one and then the other, pudgy arms stretched out in front of him for balance. I stood still for a moment, awestruck by the colours across the bay; the turquoise, blues and greens, and Carraig Fhada lighthouse far in the distance, its rectangular walls glowing a brilliant, dazzling white. Laden down with a beach umbrella, picnic basket and swimming bags, I called out to the girls for help when Bailey got dangerously close to the water. 'Come back, you little tyke!' Taylor called out as the pair of them ran towards the shoreline, giggling.

Stretching a checked blanket out over the sand, I shook my flip-flops off and sat down, smiling as the five of them dodged and criss-crossed the surf. After a picnic lunch, Bailey curled up on my lap and went to sleep, the soft skin of his feet coated in a thin layer of sand. For the next half an hour or so, Emily and Taylor collected shells while Jamie and Reece frolicked at the edge of the waves.

About halfway through the afternoon Reece and Jamie began excavating a hole, Bailey sitting on the edge with his feet dangling over the side. Every time they tossed a spade full of sand in the air the toddler glanced in my direction, shrieking with laughter. 'Boom! Sand rockets!' I said, clapping my hands together. He copied me, swinging his little chubby legs to and fro in excitement. Taylor, no longer distracted by her surroundings, sat beside me and curled her toes back and forth. 'I feel sick, Rosie,' she said, her cheeks pale and drawn.

'Come and help me build a sandcastle then,' Emily said invitingly. Even though I hadn't said much to my two, I think Emily appreciated the enormity of the situation. It was sweet, the way she had tried her best to cheer Taylor up.

Taylor sighed and stood up with a groan, as if the weight of her apprehension were too heavy a load to lift. Sitting a few feet away from me, she dug her fingers deep into the sand and clawed away as if her life depended on it. Emily, beside her, scooped up handfuls of sand and let it fall through her fingers, carefully examining the fragments of shells that remained. The pair of them were so different, their only shared interest a love of art and craft, and yet still they had become firm friends.

As the afternoon wore on and the wind picked up, the boys reluctantly dried themselves off and put on an extra layer of clothes. Taylor put her arms around my middle and rested her head on my shoulder, exhausted, I think, from all the waiting. With an expression of pained tolerance she kept glancing at her watch and then checking my phone, (the beach had been one of the few places we received a signal) positioned carefully on the blanket beside her. A bold seagull landed close by, its claws brushing the edge of our blanket. Angling its head, two black eyes considered us knowingly, as if sympathetic to our predicament. When Taylor reached out her hand, the bird hopped from foot to foot and then flew away.

It was almost four o'clock when the phone finally rang, both of us starting when it sprang into life as if we hadn't been waiting for it all afternoon. Taylor snatched it up and then screeched as if a live snake was jiggling around in her trembling, upturned hands. The caller ID read 'Max'. I took the handset with my heart in my mouth and my eyes fixed on hers, knowing that what I was about to hear would affect the three children deeply for the rest of their lives.

Chapter Twenty-Six

'You're *so* gonna cry, I know it!' Taylor trilled as we drove towards the motorway. It was the first Monday in September, two weeks after our return from Islay and we were on the move again, only this time with a handbag full of travel sickness pills and the whole-hearted support of the children seated in the back. Travel weary, Emily and Jamie had said their goodbyes after breakfast, faces streaked with tears as they went off to spend the day with their grandmother.

'Why would I cry? I'm happy for you,' I said, though feeling absorbed and far away I didn't make my usual effort to keep my tone light. There was no melodic humming under my breath, no cheery banter to and fro. In truth I could already feel my chest tightening with emotion. I hated goodbyes, and since Claire Fielding had been advised to cut all contact with her past life after winning custody of her children, I knew it was unlikely that I'd ever see or hear from them again. My eyes flicked to the rear-view mirror where I could see Bailey snoozing in his car seat. With his head resting on his soft koala toy, cheeks slightly flushed, he looked so peaceful, so innocent and sweet. Tears, I'm afraid, were inevitable; one of the pitfalls of fostering.

We drove for a long time along monotonous dual carriageways, through a fine mist of rain. Bailey slept for almost two hours, only waking when wide roads lined with cow parsley gave way to narrow winding lanes, cottages with thatched roofs nestling among the trees. Blinking as he woke, he looked sharply around and, realising he was still imprisoned by his straps, began to wail. 'Out, Mama!' he shouted. 'Want out!'

'Nearly there, my sweet,' I crooned, watching as his cheeks grew hot, eyes screwed up in mounting fury.

The women's refuge, a large Georgian detached house surrounded by several acres of land, was located in a small hamlet over two hundred miles from the children's home town. We pulled into the driveway just as Bailey's screams reached full throttle, his face a lighter shade of purple. As soon as we parked in one of the parking spaces designated for visitors, Taylor tore out of the car and ran towards the house, the cold, damp air sweeping through the open door. My heart lightened as I unstrapped Bailey and lifted him out, relieved to finally be able to comfort him. 'There we are, honey,' I said, hugging him to me and wiping his damp cheeks with my hand. 'You're free. No more car seat today.' He rubbed his cheek on my shoulder, hiccoughing as a final sob shuddered through his small body.

Torn

From the outside, the house looked grand but welcoming, the sort of place that conjured images of stories by firelight and candlelit suppers, of soft fluffy towels and warm flannel sheets. I knew it was a transient place for the Fieldings and they would soon be moving on, but I couldn't think of a nicer place for them to stay while they adjusted to life as a single parent family.

As soon as the smart, royal-blue door opened, Taylor launched herself into her mother's arms with a joyful cry, almost knocking the slight woman over. Bailey, instantly recovered, kicked his way out of my arms and bombed towards them, the pair parting with a laugh and lifting the toddler high into the air. Struck by a brief, irrational pang of jealousy, I turned swiftly back to the car to fetch all the bags. Reece, who had been watching the reunion with quiet contemplation, turned and followed me to help. He'd been downcast all morning, perhaps dreading the moment of parting as much as I was. It had been hard for him to say goodbye to Jamie; they'd been the best of buddies since that very first day in placement and, although he loved his mum, we had grown close over the past few months.

I was about to hand him a rucksack from the boot when he blew out some air and looked up at me mournfully. 'What's up, little man?' I asked, dropping the bag down on the gravel drive.

'My tummy hurts,' he said, resting his head against my arm.

I cupped a finger under his cheek and tilted his face up to mine. 'It's a lot to take in, isn't it, honey?' I said softly.

'Lots of changes in a short space of time. But it looks like a lovely place here and you're back with Mummy. That's very good news isn't it?'

He nodded without enthusiasm. 'Yes, but when do I get to see you and Jamie and Emily?' There was sadness and confusion in his voice.

'Listen,' I said, crouching down and drawing him onto my lap. 'Do you remember I told you that it might be difficult for me to see you now?' He nodded again, his chest swelling with emotion. 'Well, how about I send you a special book with photos and pictures of places we've been? Would you like that?'

'Yeah, with lots of photos of Jamie please, and your garden.'

'It's a deal,' I said, laughing over the lump in my throat.

Claire was waiting for us in the large hallway, Bailey still in her arms. Wearing a multi-coloured jumper, jeans and a hint of make-up, she looked bright and cheerful, much happier than the last time I'd seen her. For years she had lived her life as the shadow of a person, the only way she could possibly survive. Now, she was free to begin the family life she'd always wanted.

She helped us pile the bags up in the corner of the hall and then leaned forward to kiss me on the cheek. Bailey reached out and wrapped his arms around my neck, Claire releasing him into my arms for a cuddle. I began to feel a little sick. The toddler cupped his hands around my face and, feeling the urge to cry, I jerked my head playfully, pretending to gobble him up. Giggling riotously, he dug his heels into my sides and tried to climb up my trunk, his chest resting against my face. I blew a raspberry on his tummy and then briskly handed him back to Claire. Abruptly, tears appeared on my cheeks.

'Oh, Rosie, I'm sorry,' Claire said, her eyes filling sympathetically. She reached out and grabbed my hand. 'I can't tell you how grateful I am.'

'I knew it!' Taylor said triumphantly as she ran back into the hallway from an unseen room. 'She's such a wimp, Mum, she cries at everything,' she said, but her voice was slightly hoarse and when I turned to give her a hug she held onto me tight. When we pulled apart there were tears rolling down her cheeks. She swiped at them as if they were poisonous insects and I laughed, patting my eyes with the back of my wrist.

Driving away, I was surprised to find that the sadness I felt knowing I would never see the children again was punctuated with faint twinges of regret. With thoughts of our long days out through the warm spring and early summer, afternoon walks along the riverbank and late evenings sitting in the garden, I found myself wishing I had made the most of the time they'd spent with me. I remembered the joy of watching as they frolicked around on the grass, peeling off their socks and running through the sprinkler, laughing helplessly as they chased each other around. And then the triumphs: Reece's pride at becoming dry at night, Taylor's delight when she received her first birthday party invitation.

Had Taylor really been so impregnable, I wondered later, as I let myself into my empty home, or had my inexperience stood in the way of really getting to know her? Apart from being redundant, I supposed the question was really impossible to answer. Viewed through the protective film of the past, when the responsibility had been stripped away and the house was orderly and neat (and dare I say, just a little too peaceful) it was easy to look back with rose-tinted spectacles. When foster children moved on, there was a tendency for my mind to retouch the memory of them, airbrushing out the difficulties. Perhaps it was a little like childbirth in that way.

I suddenly thought of a fridge magnet my mother had given me soon after I began fostering, featuring a mother and two young children. In the picture, the mother leans over the youngsters, wagging her finger at them, the caption below reading: 'Now, remember, as far as anyone knows, we're a normal family.'

The gift struck a chord and made me smile, as my mother knew it would. Sometimes I worried that Emily and Jamie's upbringing may have been a little dysfunctional, with me being a single parent and troubled children floating in and out of their lives. But then again, almost every other mother I knew (outside of fostering) seemed to exhaust themselves in pursuit of the perfect existence for their children. After-school clubs, private tuition, educational trips and games – some ran themselves ragged, trying to fit it all in. And then there was the minefield of the internet to worry about, with all its hidden dangers: cyber-bullying, chatrooms and online porn. Were computer games damaging their cognitive ability? What about the impact of watching too much TV, or not enough?

Witnessing Taylor, Reece and Bailey's total contentment at being back in their mother's arms, even though the family had little else to their name, was a powerful antidote to that internal monologue of guilt. It made me stop and think, at least for a short while – who do we do it all for, when all children really need is the certain knowledge that they are loved?

Claire wasn't a perfect mother by any stretch of the imagination, if such a being actually existed, but she offered her children a strong sense of identity, belonging and, most importantly, unconditional, maternal love. In that respect, viewed from any angle, she was undoubtedly the best person for the job.

Epilogue

Back in 2005, I hadn't yet learned to overwrite the unthinkable thoughts that fostering can sometimes arouse and so, remembering what Maisie had said about the first few weeks after a woman has made the break from an abusive relationship being the most dangerous, for a while following the children's departure, I felt uneasy every time they entered my thoughts. I told myself that there were some expert advisors on hand at the refuge, but it seemed that every time I switched on the news, there were reminders of the precariousness of their situation, with photos of smiling young women appearing on screen, blissfully unaware of the fate awaiting them. And then the depressingly paltry sentences handed out to their murderous lovers, as if dying at the hands of someone they trusted were less of a crime.

One day, in mid-October, yet another disturbing story made the headlines, this time a husband who had murdered his children but spared his wife, the reprieve his way of maximising her suffering. Shuddering, I switched the TV off in disgust, another ripple of anxiety running through me.

But about two weeks later, eight weeks after the placement had ended, there was an unexpected knock at the door. I answered it to find a young, attractive woman with long, glossy black hair standing on the doorstep. 'Sorry to call unannounced,' she said, eyeing my surprise with amusement.

'Oh my goodness! Sorry, Maisie,' I said, pointedly running my hands down my own hair. 'I hardly recognised you without the –'

She laughed. 'No, it's taken a few people by surprise. I've got some news, Rosie, something I didn't want to discuss over the phone.'

I ushered her in, my pulse jumping around as I wondered what might have happened. 'Are they OK?' I asked, before we'd reached the living room.

Maisie smiled and I felt my heart rate returning to normal. 'So, right, everything's cool. I've been up to see them to make a final welfare visit and they're doing really well. Taylor and Reece have made some friends at their new school and they've moved into a place of their own. It's small but comfortable and they have their own garden.'

I put my hand to my chest. 'Ah, that's wonderful news.'

'They asked me to give you this,' Maisie said on her way out, her eyes twinkling as she handed me an envelope.

After waving her off I turned the letter over in my hand, smiling at the tiny fairies Taylor had drawn along on the back of the seal. I opened it and took out a handmade card, pale blue, with a dog drawn on the front and pink hearts around the edges. Inside, Taylor had written a message in small, neat script:

Dear Rosie

How's Emily? I know you can't write me back but we wanted to let you know that we're not at the place you took us no more. We're in a new house and I've got my own room! Mum made Reece share with Bailey, ha ha! And guess what? It's the best news ever … we're getting a puppy. I won't love him as much as Jimmy but he'll be super cute I bet. I wish I could show him to you.

Love from Taylor

PS Reece and Bailey are missing you. They send you big squishy hugs xxx

Apart from the joy of looking after children, one of the best things about fostering was seeing hope rising out of turmoil. Away from the brooding chaos that every day brought, Taylor and her siblings had, at long last, been given the chance to live a normal, peaceful and happy life. As long as Claire kept to her word and stayed away from Myspace and other technology, it was unlikely that Nick would ever find them again.

Wiping happy tears from my face with the sleeve of my cardigan, I rested the card on the mantelpiece for Emily and Jamie to see when they got home from school.

ALSO AVAILABLE

The struggle to escape a life defined by family honour

With Rosie's support, 13-year-old Zadie gradually begins to settle into her new surroundings. But loyalty to her relatives and fear of bringing shame on her family keeps preventing Zadie from confessing the horrifying truth about her past. Will Rosie be able to persuade her to open up in time?

BETRAYED

ROSIE LEWIS

Trapped

The terrifying
true story of a
young girl's secret
world of abuse

The terrifying true story of a secret world of abuse

Phoebe, an autistic nine-year-old girl, is taken into
care when a chance comment to one of her teachers
alerts the authorities. After several shocking incidents
of self-harming and threats to kill, experienced foster
carer Rosie Lewis begins to suspect that there is
much more to Phoebe's horrific past than she
could ever have imagined.

TRAPPED

AVAILABLE AS E-BOOK ONLY

ROSIE LEWIS

Helpless

A true story

An abandoned baby girl

Rosie is called to look after a new baby, born to an addict mother on a freezing cold December night, and to care for her until she can meet her forever family.

HELPLESS

ROSIE LEWIS

A Small Boy's Cry

A true story

Toddler Charlie is found after falling from a second-floor window

Once he is taken into care, Rosie helps terrified Charlie open up and uncovers his traumatic past.

A SMALL BOY'S CRY

Found beneath a bench, seemingly alone

Angell comes into the home and heart of foster carer Rosie Lewis. Will Angell be destined to spend the rest of her childhood in care or will her mother return for her?

TWO MORE SLEEPS

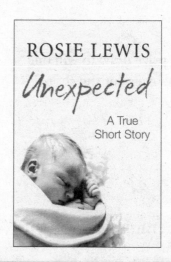

Ellen is so shocked by the sudden birth of her baby girl that she abandons the newborn in hospital

Rosie struggles to understand how anyone can treat a baby in this way, but with time she begins to see the dark secret Ellen is hiding.

UNEXPECTED

Moving Memoirs

Stories of hope, courage and the power of love…

If you loved this book, then you will love our Moving Memoirs eNewsletter

Sign up to…

- Be the first to hear about new books

- Get sneak previews from your favourite authors

- Read exclusive interviews

- Be entered into our monthly prize draw to win one of our latest releases before it's even hit the shops!

Sign up at

www.moving-memoirs.com